LEARNING FROM THE GIANTS

Books by Dr. John C. Maxwell
Can Teach You How to Be a REAL Success

Relationships

25 Ways to Win with People

Becoming a Person of Influence

Encouragement Changes Everything

Ethics 101

Everyone Communicates, Few Connect

The Power of Partnership

Relationships 101

Winning with People

Attitude

Attitude 101

The Difference Maker

Failing Forward

How Successful People Think

Sometimes You Win, Sometimes You Learn

Success 101

Thinking for a Change

The Winning Attitude

Equipping

The 15 Invaluable Laws of Growth

The 17 Essential Qualities of a Team Player

The 17 Indisputable Laws of Teamwork

Developing the Leaders Around You

How Successful People Grow

Equipping 101

Make Today Count

Mentoring 101

My Dream Map

Partners in Prayer

Put Your Dream to the Test

Running with the Giants

Talent Is Never Enough

Today Matters

Your Road Map for Success

Leadership

The 21 Irrefutable Laws of Leadership, 10th Anniversary Edition

The 21 Indispensable Qualities of a Leader

The 21 Most Powerful Minutes in a Leader's Day

The 360 Degree Leader

Developing the Leader Within You

The 5 Levels of Leadership

Go for Gold

Good Leaders Ask Great Questions

How Successful People Lead

Leadership 101

Leadership Gold

Leadership Promises for Every Day

LEARNING FROM THE GIANTS

LIFE AND LEADERSHIP LESSONS FROM THE BIBLE

JOHN C. MAXWELL

NEW YORK BOSTON NASHVILLE

The author is represented by Yates & Yates, LLP, Literary Agency,
Orange, California.

All Scripture references are NIV unless otherwise noted.

FaithWords
Hachette Book Group
1290 Avenue of the Americas
New York, NY 10104

faithwords.com

Printed in the United States of America

RRD-C

First Edition: November 2014
10 9 8 7 6 5 4 3 2 1

FaithWords is a division of Hachette Book Group, Inc.
The FaithWords name and logo are trademarks of Hachette Book Group, Inc.

The Hachette Speakers Bureau provides a wide range of authors for
speaking events. To find out more, go to www.hachettespeakersbureau.com
or call (866) 376-6591.

The publisher is not responsible for websites (or their content)
that are not owned by the publisher.

Library of Congress Cataloging-in-Publication Data

Maxwell, John C., 1947–
    Learning from the giants : life and leadership lessons from the Bible / John C.
Maxwell. — First Edition.
        pages cm
    Includes bibliographical references.
    ISBN 978-1-4555-5707-3 (hardcover) — ISBN 978-1-4555-5706-6 (ebook) —
ISBN 978-1-4789-8297-5 (audiobook) — ISBN 978-1-4789-8298-2
(audio download) — ISBN 978-1-4555-3125-7 (spanish trade pbk.) —
ISBN 978-1-4555-3127-1 (spanish ebook)   1. Christian life—Biblical
teaching.   2. Leadership—Religious aspects—Christianity.   3. Bible. Old
Testament—Biography.   I. Title.
    BS1199.C43M39 2014
    221.9'22—dc23
                                                        2014012999

To the people of Christ Fellowship Church. You inspired me to preach about these giants of the faith. I love you. Thank you for accepting me and allowing me to be one of your pastors.

CONTENTS

ACKNOWLEDGMENTS

I'd like to say thank you to:

Charlie Wetzel, my writer

Audrey Moralez, who researched and contributed her great ideas

Carolyn Kokinda, who typed the first chapter drafts

Stephanie Wetzel, who reviewed and edited the manuscript

Linda Eggers, my executive assistant

LEARNING FROM THE GIANTS

MENTORS FOR
A DAY

Imagine you could spend a day being mentored by some of the giants of the faith, the men and women of the Old Testament who fought and won great battles, served kings, endured great hardship for God, and came out on the other side transformed. What if they could sit down in a chair across from you, and you had the privilege of spending a few precious minutes with each of them? What would that be like?

That was the intriguing idea that drove me to write this book.

I have been studying the leaders of the Bible for more than fifty years. Truth be told, everything I know about leadership has come from Scripture. I shared some of the insights I gained about life and leadership in *Running with the Giants*. For many years, people have been asking me to write another book like it. I've spent another ten years reading, meditating on, and studying the major figures of the Bible. And I'm finally ready to share what I've learned.

So come along with me as I imagine what it would be like to meet nine giants of the faith, each spending a few minutes to share the lessons he or she has learned about life and leadership.

ELIJAH

God Loves You on Your Bad Days

It's a few minutes before dawn—my favorite time of day—and my home is completely silent. I meet you at my front door and welcome you in. Together we walk down the long hallway and enter my study.

I glance at my desk. The most recent outline for a lesson that I've been working on sits there partly finished, a stack of quote cards next to it. It will require at most only another hour of my time. I leave it alone. I will work on it tomorrow. Today we are going to experience something I've been looking forward to for months. Today we will be mentored by some of the giants of the faith. I don't know who will be coming. I only know that in a few minutes they will begin arriving, one by one, and spend a few minutes with us sharing their wisdom.

My sense of anticipation is off the charts. This is going to be a spectacular day. Together we will learn from people who have experienced moments with God that changed their lives—and this has the potential to change ours. I am so glad you have decided to join me.

We look outside and we can see that the sun is peeking its head above the horizon and turning the sky above the Atlantic Ocean different shades of pink, orange, and red. It's glorious. I move toward my favorite overstuffed armchair, where I often sit to pray and think. It's surrounded by some of my favorite things: a photograph of my father and me teaching together when he was ninety, the handful of books that have made the greatest impact on my life, and several favorite items from my John Wesley collection.

The view of the ocean is spectacular. I invite you to settle in beside me in the comfortable chair that matches my own. A third chair, positioned across from us, is empty. We sit silently, wondering who will be the first to arrive and meet with us.

We don't have to wait long.

We can hear someone walking up the hallway, the sound of leather soles gently treading on the stone floor. And then he's standing in the doorway—a bald man neither young nor old. He wears a plain tunic with a leather belt. On his shoulders rests a camel-hair cloak. We can see that, near the neck, there is an odd-shaped tear in the cloak that shows signs of having been repaired.

The man's expression is intense, serious. I wonder who this might be.

"I was a man of great influence in my country," he says, eyeing us intently as he walks over and settles into the chair opposite us. "I had the confidence of the people, the ear of the king, and the power of God. I condemned King Ahab, the most wicked of Israel's kings. I prophesied the three-year drought. And I proved to everyone that Baal was an impotent false god, worthy of nothing but contempt."

Of course. It's Elijah. We are face-to-face with Elijah!

This Old Testament prophet stood up to Ahab, the king who was said to have sold himself to do evil and who did more to provoke God than all the other kings of Israel before him. Ahab married Jezebel, who brought Baal worship to Israel and urged Ahab to abandon God and chase false gods. When Ahab built altars and temples to these false gods, Elijah told the wicked king that a drought would settle on Israel until Elijah declared that it would end. Ahab and Jezebel became so furious that they wanted to kill Elijah, and the prophet had to flee. But God took care of him, first by having ravens bring him food and then by leading him to a widow in Zarephath whose flour and oil were miraculously replenished so that Elijah, the widow, and her son could stay fed.

"I have something important to tell you," Elijah says as he fixes us with his eyes. *"God loves you on your bad days."*

The Best of Days

I'm surprised to hear Elijah talk about bad days, because he was at the center of one of the greatest days in Israel's history. After three long years of drought, God told Elijah to present himself to Ahab because God was finally going to make it rain. But first Elijah was going to show all of Israel that God is God and that Baal, the supposed god of fertility and rain, was nothing.

It was a great day because…

1. God Chose Elijah for This Important Assignment

God had chosen Elijah to tell Ahab there would be a drought three years before, but that didn't mean He had to choose Elijah again—but He did. He invited Elijah to perform one of the greatest miracles ever witnessed on earth.

2. Elijah Fearlessly Obeyed God

It took courage for Elijah to face Israel's king and tell him that he was to blame for the nation's problems. It took boldness for Elijah to tell Ahab to summon Jezebel's favorites, the 850 false prophets of Baal and Asherah, to Mount Carmel. It took confidence for him to challenge Baal's prophets to summon fire from their god to burn their sacrifice and mock them when they shouted and danced and cut themselves in their vain attempt to do so.

3. Elijah Boldly Believed God

When Baal's servants failed, Elijah demonstrated the boldness of his faith in God by having the ox and firewood on his altar drenched three times in water. And he demonstrated no doubt when he asked God to make Himself known by bringing fire down upon the sacrifice. And of course God delivered, consuming not only the animal and the wood, but also the water, the dirt, and even the stone. God's actions won over the people of Israel, who proclaimed, "The Lord—He is God!" and slew all the false prophets at Elijah's command.

4. God Strengthened Elijah

After God showed his power on Mount Carmel, Elijah waited for God to bring rain, and when it came, there was a mighty storm. King Ahab raced in his chariot to Jezreel to keep from getting stuck in the mud, but Elijah, strengthened by God, was able to tuck his robe into his belt and *run* to Jezreel ahead of Ahab—a distance of seventeen miles!

"The day God used me to bring fire down to consume the sacrifice and scourge the land of the false prophets was the greatest day of my life," Elijah explains. "You must understand: the entire nation had turned their backs on God. After the miracle on Mount Carmel, I believed they would no longer be able to deny Him. My heart longed for people to turn back to God." Elijah's voice cracks as he says the words, and he falls silent for a moment.

The Worst of Days

"When I got back to Jezreel, I was ecstatic. God had called me, gifted me, and incredibly blessed me. He had used me greatly and I had fulfilled His will!" Elijah continues. "I assumed that everything would be changed after that, that only good things would happen. After all, I had obeyed God. But soon my assumption was shattered.

"Ahab told Jezebel everything that had happened, including the death of her beloved false prophets," Elijah says, his shoulders slumping as the memory seems to weigh on him. "Jezebel immediately sent a messenger who said she had vowed to kill me." Elijah's head drops into his hands.

"I assumed that my days of conflict with Jezebel would be over—they weren't.

"I assumed that the people of Israel would only worship the one true God—they didn't.

"I assumed that my ministry with God would always be spectacular—it wasn't.

"So I ran," Elijah says flatly. "All my courage left me. After a few days, I even left behind my servant, who would have helped me. I went into the desert to die alone," Elijah continues. "The best of days had turned into the worst of days. I told God I'd had enough and asked Him to take my life."

Life Lessons from Elijah

Elijah sits silently. Now I begin to understand. The fall must have felt twice as great because Elijah had fallen from such a height. No wonder he had felt so discouraged. But then Elijah's expression changes. "But even on our worst days, God still loves us," he says. "You would do well to understand these truths..."

"God Can Never Be Disappointed in Us"

"I was crushed. Here I was, a prophet of the Lord God Almighty, yet I had fled to Beersheba. When I lay down under the broom tree, I wanted to die. I was no better than my ancestors. What a failure. I was so disappointed in myself. But God was not disappointed in me. He never has been, nor will He ever be disappointed in you.

"Disappointment comes when reality falls short of our expectations. But nothing falls short of God's expectations because He knows *everything*. We cannot surprise Him. Don't put your disappointment in yourself on God. He does not see us through our eyes. He sees us through His own. He loves us and wants the best for us."

> *Disappointment comes when reality falls short of our expectations. But nothing falls short of God's expectations because He knows everything.*

"God Will Nourish Us When We Have Nothing"

"When I fell asleep under the broom tree waiting to die, God sent an angel to care for me, giving me food and water. I should have known that God would do this; He had fed me before using ravens and the poor widow. God's provision made me strong again, strong enough to walk forty days and nights, all the way to Horeb, the mountain of God. When you feel desperate and you have nothing, look to God. He will care for you."

"God Will Connect with Us When We Feel Alone"

"When I got to the cave at Mount Horeb, I felt utterly alone. I thought I was the only person in all of Israel who still worshipped God. But God did not let me stay alone. He invited me to connect with Him by asking me a question: 'What are you doing here, Elijah?' That's all I needed to pour my heart out to Him. God understood me, even when I didn't understand Him or myself. Before my experience on Mount Horeb, I thought I knew God. When He sent fire down on Mount Carmel, I thought, *That's God!* So I expected Him to always show Himself in power. But He wasn't in the mighty winds or the earthquake or even fire that day. He spoke in a whisper.

"God turned my loneliness, my feelings of emptiness and self-pity, into aloneness, a sense of fulfillment and contentment. On Mount Carmel, God showed up for everyone else. At Mount Horeb, He showed up for me. At Mount Carmel, God was spectacular to everyone. At Mount Horeb, He was special to me."

If you let Him, God will connect with you. We want God to do the spectacular every time, but sometimes He would rather whisper to

> *We want God to do the spectacular every time, but sometimes He would rather whisper to us.*

us. And when we do connect with God, we want Him to connect with us again in the same way every time. But there's always more to God, and He likes to make things new. We may not always know *how* He will connect with us, but we can be certain that He always *wants* to connect with us.

"Even When We Give Up on Ourselves, God Will Not Give Up on Us"

If you forget everything else I tell you, please remember this: you never have to doubt God because He loves you fully and completely, even knowing you are flawed and weak. You may believe that you deserve or don't deserve something because of your failure, but I can tell you from firsthand experience: God loves you just as much under the broom tree as He does on Mount Carmel.

"I could not return to my ministry until I learned this and regained my perspective. I could not regain my perspective until I could hear God. I could not hear God until I was quiet and alone. No matter what has happened in your life, return to God. He has not given up on you, and He never will. God is faithful to the end."

> *No matter what has happened in your life, return to God. He has not given up on you, and He never will. God is faithful to the end.*

Elijah's Prayer for Us

Suddenly Elijah stands up. We get ready to stand up too, but before we can, Elijah says, "The Lord has asked me to pray for you," and he places a hand on each of our heads.

> *"Lord God Almighty,*
> *"Put the fire of Your Spirit into Your servants.*
> *Show Your power to the world through them as You*
> *did through me on Mount Carmel. When they have*
> *bad days and feel discouraged, speak to them in*
> *Your gentle whisper and encourage them. Amen."*

Leadership Lessons from Elijah

The room resonates with the sound of Elijah's voice. Only now do we feel we've really heard and understood him. There was power in his prayer. When we open our eyes, he is gone.

There are so many questions we could have asked him. I'm struck by his experience and his insights. I have experienced highs and lows in my life and leadership. I'm sure you have too. None of my highs were as high as his, but neither were any of my lows as low as what he experienced.

There are many leadership lessons we can learn from Elijah, but three stand out to me as I reflect on what he said to us:

1. Even God's Best Leaders Are Human

It's very easy for us to read the Bible and believe that the great leaders whose stories we read were somehow beyond life's normal trials, temptations, and failures. We want to see these giants of the faith as superhuman, but they were not. Their gifts were greater than they were. And they were asked to do things beyond their own capacity. They were in many ways ordinary men and women, but they served an extraordinary God!

> We want to see these giants of the faith as superhuman, but they were not. Their gifts were greater than they were.

2. Leaders Make the Greatest Impact When They Lead

As obvious as it may sound, leaders must remember that they make a positive difference when they lead. As leaders, we can get caught up in many things that aren't the main thing. Elijah was at his best when he was leading on Mount Carmel. Good leaders remain focused on what God has called them to do.

3. God's Desire for Discouraged Leaders Is for Them to Get Back into Leadership

Every leader fails. Every leader becomes discouraged at some time. Every leader becomes disappointed and wants to run away or quit. Often other people look at a leader's failure and think, *They've blown it. They are disqualified from ever leading again.*

But that's not how God thinks. When these things happen, what is God's desire for these leaders? He wants them to be restored to Him and to get back into the game. After God connected with Elijah and restored their relationship, He told Elijah to go back the way he came, because He still had things for him to do. We should continue to serve God in whatever way He asks. We're not finished until He says so.

Elijah's Discussion Guide

The Lord said, "Go out and stand on the mountain in the presence of the Lord, for the Lord is about to pass by." Then a great and powerful wind tore the mountains apart and shattered the rocks before the Lord, but the Lord was not in the wind. After the wind there was an earthquake, but the Lord was not in the earthquake. After the earthquake came a fire, but the Lord was not in the fire. And after the fire came a gentle whisper. When Elijah heard it, he pulled his cloak over his face and went out and stood at the mouth of the cave. (1 Kings 19:11–13)

1. Do you identify with Elijah? If so, in what ways?
2. Have you ever felt compelled to share a hard truth with another person? If so, how did it turn out?
3. Have you ever personally experienced a time when God showed Himself to you in a significant way?
4. Have you ever been so discouraged that you felt totally alone?
5. Have you ever allowed your disappointment in yourself to make you think God was disappointed in you? Explain. What was the impact?

6. How do you go about trying to hear the gentle whisper of God? What percentage of the time do you feel successful?
7. What are you willing to do this week to pursue God and get better connected to Him?

To learn more about Elijah, read 1 Kings 17:1–19:21 and 21:1–29, and 2 Kings 1:1–2:12.

ELISHA

Give Your Best Wherever God Puts You

Elijah has been gone from the room for a while, but the impact of his presence continues to linger. What a powerful man. We can tell that we have been in the presence of a giant of the faith. So I'm surprised when I look up and realize that the next mentor is already in the room, waiting for us to greet him. I wonder why we didn't hear him coming.

He is dressed in worn but sturdy work clothes, the kind of things a laborer might wear in the fields. There's nothing fancy about him. He has a no-nonsense look about him, and he appears to be ordinary in every way. He looks lean, sinewy, and strong, like he's worked hard every day of his life. His face is weather-beaten and sunburned.

I'm surprised to see that he wears a camel-hair cloak just like Elijah's. Then I notice an oddly shaped repair at the neck of the cloak. I saw the same thing on Elijah's cloak, and that's when it hits me. His isn't *like* Elijah's cloak. This *is* Elijah's cloak! There's only one person this could be: Elisha. Scripture says Elisha received Elijah's mantle or cloak before Elijah was taken up into heaven.

"Have you ever felt insignificant, overlooked, and underappreciated?" he asks us as he sits. We both nod a yes. "I have too. The day Elijah brought fire down upon the sacrifice on Mount Carmel, I was at work in my father's fields. I didn't see it, but I heard about it. Everyone did. It was a great day for Israel, a great day for God, and a great day for Elijah.

"One day after it happened, I was out plowing in the field and Elijah came and placed his mantle around my shoulders. I couldn't believe it," Elisha says. "When my master chose me to succeed him as prophet, I knew I was exchanging my old life for a new one. The life of a farmer for the life of God's servant. I expected to do great things even that very day! But I didn't. Instead, for the next ten years I followed Elijah around and worked as a common servant. I felt insignificant.

"When we choose to follow God, what we get doesn't always match what we expected. No matter. Even if others ignore or

> *Whatever you're doing for God is important to God.*

forget you, whatever you're doing *for* God is important *to* God. For that reason," Elisha admonishes, "*give your best wherever God puts you.*"

When You Give Your Best

I turn Elisha's words over in my mind. It's true that God's ways are not our ways. What we want isn't always what serves God best. Yet when we are willing to put ourselves in God's hands and do what He asks, giving our best, God uses us. Even before Elisha begins to speak again, I'm starting to understand some things about the way God works:

1. If You Give Your Best in Obscurity, God Will Recognize It

When Elijah complained that he was the only one left among the Israelites who was zealous for the Lord God Almighty, God told him He had reserved seven thousand who remained true to Him. Elisha was one of those seven thousand. An anonymous farmer, Elisha worked in obscurity, following God and remaining loyal to him. After he was designated Elijah's successor, for a decade he again worked in obscurity.

When we receive a call from God, we are often anxious to begin the work immediately. No doubt Elisha wanted to be God's prophet. But God often gives us the time we need to learn what we must to serve Him well, even if it's not what we want. In the case of Elisha, serving Elijah helped him learn how to serve God. Elisha left a season of sowing in the fields to enter a season of sowing in the life of Elijah.

This reminds me of something I once read by author and theologian Richard Foster: "More than any other single way—the grace of humility is worked into our lives through the discipline of service...nothing disciplines the inordinate desires of the flesh like service, and nothing transforms the desires of the flesh like serving in hiddenness. The flesh whines against service but it screams against hidden service. It strains and pulls for honor and recognition." If Elisha wanted to rail against hidden service, there is no indication in Scripture that he did it.

2. If You Do Your Best in the Small Things, God Will Give You Bigger Things to Do

In the ten years Elisha served Elijah, he was asked to do the lowliest of tasks. An officer of the king of Israel described Elisha as the one who used to pour water on the hands of Elijah. That was normally the job of a servant of low status. If Elisha did that, he undoubtedly performed other menial tasks during his decade of service.

This was undoubtedly a change for Elisha. When Elijah placed his mantle on him, Elisha had been plowing with twelve yoke of oxen. That means his family must have been wealthy. It is likely that he was used to having others serve him. But Elisha was willing to do whatever God asked of him.

> *If you are willing to do small things in the service of God, and do them with excellence, God will give you opportunities to do bigger things for Him when you are ready.*

If you are willing to do small things in the service of God, and do them with excellence, God will give you opportunities to do bigger things for Him when you are ready.

3. If You Give Your Best with Consistency, God Will Give You Courage

Elisha served faithfully and with consistency. That gave him courage. When he knew Elijah was about to be taken from him, Elisha asked for a double portion of his spirit.

This was a huge request from Elisha. For ten years he had done nothing but menial tasks. When most people are used to doing small things, they can't see themselves as capable of great ones. But Elisha could. He had the courage to ask, but he was requesting twice the ability of Israel's greatest prophet!

Maybe Elijah didn't believe Elisha was capable of great things. Perhaps that's why Elijah told him he had asked a difficult thing, and why he tried to separate himself from his protégé. Three different times Elijah asked Elisha to stay behind while the older prophet went on. Three times Elisha went with him. He wanted Elijah's blessing. And because of his consistency, tenacity, and faithfulness, he got it.

When we serve God faithfully, doing what He asks us to do with consistency, then when God invites us to do bigger things, we should not shrink back. Instead we should be bold and think big, as Elisha did. We should never allow the size of our thinking to limit the size of our vision. Our God is way too big for that.

4. If You Give Your Best for His Glory, God Will Empower You to Do Things Greater Than Your Ability

Elisha was a farmer. Plowing, sowing, watering, harvesting—all of these were things he was capable of doing. But what did he actually end up doing? He performed miracles! He fed hundreds with a few loaves of bread, purified bad water, made an axhead float, healed the diseased, and raised the dead. Not only did Elisha do more than he was capable of doing on his own, but he actually did more than his master Elijah had. He had double the spirit and did twice as many miracles as his predecessor. Elijah did fourteen miracles, but Elisha did twenty-eight.

Life Lessons from Elisha

Elisha clears his throat to get our attention, and he begins to speak again:

"Give Yourself Completely to the Task at Hand"

"Whatever task God gave me I did with all my heart and all my ability. When I plowed, I worked long and hard making furrows straight and ready for seed. I encouraged the workers under me and urged them to do the same.

"When I served Elijah, I did everything I could to help him. No task was beneath me. No task was ever left undone. Helping him fulfill God's vision was my purpose.

"And when God raised me up to be His prophet, I

did everything He asked me to do. What you do doesn't determine whether your work is sacred. How and why you do it does."

> *What you do doesn't determine whether your work is sacred. How and why you do it does.*

"Your Purpose Must Be More Important Than Your Position"

"God does not care about anyone's position. If He did, Jesus would never have put on human flesh and lived as an ordinary man. What impresses God is our faithfulness to the purpose He gives us. He was just as pleased with me when I was plowing or serving as He was when I was preaching. When you work with excellence and the right motives, God is pleased."

"When God Does Not Give You a Vision of Your Own, Help Other Leaders Fulfill Theirs"

"When God called me, I did not yet know what He would have me do. He did not give me a vision, like those He gave to Jacob or Joseph. At first the only thing He asked me to do was the task at hand. And that pleased Him.

"If God has not given you a vision, don't wait around

for one. Serve another leader to whom God *has* given a vision. Be faithful and effective in that. The person who serves behind the scenes is also honored by God."

Elisha's Prayer for Us

Before we know what's happening, Elisha is praying for us:

"O God Our Provider,

"I ask that You would encourage my friends when they feel unappreciated, empower them when they feel weary, give them courage when their motive is to serve You, and give them strength when the fulfillment of Your calling on their lives feels as if it's still a long way off. Amen."

We open our eyes and lift our heads, expecting to get one more look at Elisha, but we're too late. He's already gone. He has left as quickly and as quietly as he came.

Leadership Lessons from Elisha

Elijah was impressive. His personality filled the room when he spoke to us. Elisha was different. The power was certainly there, under the surface. But in a roomful of people, we might have missed Elisha if we didn't know who he was. I suspect that we can often be too much like Samuel when he was looking at the sons of Jesse. We put too much emphasis on appearance, and not enough on the heart, the way God does.

There are so many lessons we can learn from Elisha:

1. To Receive God's Mantle of Leadership, You Must Desire It

When Elijah placed his mantle on Elisha in the field, Elisha stopped farming, burned his plow, and followed Elijah. He showed that he not only desired to be Elijah's successor, but was willing to change his life in order to pursue this goal. That desire and attitude impresses God, and He ultimately rewards it.

I think back on my own life and see the importance of the desire to serve. Many great leaders prayed for me over the years: E. Stanley Jones, my dad, Bill Bright, Dr. Cho. I wanted their blessing as much as Elisha wanted Elijah's. I wanted to make a difference for God. I still do. If you desire to lead for God's glory, fuel your passion and pursue God's calling with all your heart.

2. To Receive God's Mantle of Leadership, You Must Be Willing to Wait for It

Elisha was willing to wait, serve, and learn before he led. And in the ten years he was Elijah's assistant, learn Elisha did. He went on to perform every kind of miracle he had watched Elijah perform—and even some he hadn't witnessed.

Even at the end, just before he received Elijah's mantle, Elisha still waited. He stayed with his master until there was nothing else he could do for him. He was content to wait for God's timing in order to assume his new role as Elijah's successor.

God's purpose works only with God's timing.

God's purpose works only with God's timing. We usually want what God has for us right now. But our desire to lead for God is really only as great as our willingness to wait on Him. Be patient.

3. To Receive God's Mantle of Leadership, You Must Stick with It

Elisha had multiple opportunities to walk away from his master, but he persevered and was faithful to Elijah and to his calling. Despite obstacles and distractions, Elisha stayed true to both God and Elijah.

Too often we look at leadership from a short-term perspective instead of a long-term one. Serving God through leadership is a marathon, not a sprint. The greater your calling, the greater the temptations and potential distractions that will come to prevent you from fulfilling it. We need to persevere. It's the only way we will be able to finish well, as Elisha did.

Elisha's Discussion Guide

Elijah took his cloak, rolled it up and struck the water with it. The water divided to the right and to the left, and the two of them crossed over on dry ground.

When they had crossed, Elijah said to Elisha, "Tell me, what can I do for you before I am taken from you?"

"Let me inherit a double portion of your spirit," Elisha replied.

"You have asked a difficult thing," Elijah said, "yet if you see me when I am taken from you, it will be yours—otherwise, it will not."

As they were walking along and talking together, suddenly a chariot of fire and horses of fire appeared and separated the two of them, and Elijah went up to heaven in a whirlwind....

Elisha then picked up Elijah's cloak that had fallen from him and went back and stood on the bank of the Jordan. He took the cloak that had fallen from Elijah and struck the water with it.... When he struck the water, it divided to the right and to the left, and he crossed over.

> The company of the prophets from Jericho,
> who were watching, said, "The spirit of Elijah is
> resting on Elisha." (2 Kings 2:8–15)

1. How do you think Elisha felt serving Elijah for so long without recognition?
2. What is your attitude when it comes to doing menial tasks for others? Explain.
3. Does knowing that your work contributes to a greater purpose help you to do tasks that you don't enjoy? If so, how are you able to encourage yourself to be faithful in your work?
4. How do you usually handle having to wait for something?
5. Has God revealed the purpose for your life, or are you in a season like Elisha's early years where God is only revealing immediate tasks for you to do? How do you feel about the season you're in?
6. If God has not given you a personal vision, have you found someone you can help who has been called to a purpose? If so, who? If not, are you willing to find someone?
7. Do you find it easy or difficult to give your best where you are? Explain.
8. What must you do to be more like Elisha?

To learn more about Elisha, read 1 Kings 19:15–21 and 2 Kings 2:1–8:15, 9:1–3, and 13:14–20.

JOB

God Sees the Big Picture

The first indication that the next person is approaching is the faint sound of footsteps. Around the corner comes a small man, less than five feet tall. He wears a robe that is spectacular. It's a vibrant green and shimmers as he walks, the light reflecting off the smooth fabric. It occurs to me that it's made of silk. He wears shoes that look like they are made of the same fabric. No wonder his footfalls were so quiet.

I look more closely at the man's robe and I see that there are gold threads running through the fabric. The way the light hits them makes me certain that the thread is made of real gold. It's stunning.

Around the man's neck is a golden chain unlike anything I've ever seen, even in a museum. The thousands of small links are woven in a beautiful elaborate pattern.

Every three inches in the chain is set a golden medallion studded with emeralds, sapphires, and rubies. I cannot imagine what something like that is worth. Every finger on his hands has a ring on it. Each is of a different design. Many of them also are adorned with gems.

I marvel at the rings. And that's when I notice the scars. They cover the backs of the man's hands and continue up his arms to where they disappear into the sleeves of his robe.

As the man sits down, I see that his ankles, exposed as he sits, are also scarred. We look him up and down and see that his face is too. Everywhere skin is visible we see faded pink and purple scars. But the worst scars are on his hands. *What could have caused that?* I wonder.

"I see you look at my rings," he says. "They were given to me by my brothers and sisters, each one a gift after God restored me from my trials. You see, Satan tortured me in the land of Uz, but I did not give up on God. My name is Job."

His words startle me. *Tortured by Satan.* But how else would you describe what happened to Job? When God pointed out to Satan that Job was a good man—blameless, upright, God-fearing, and shunning evil—Satan wanted to challenge God. Satan said Job would curse God if he lost everything he had. So God withdrew His protection from

Job and let Satan destroy everything in Job's life. When Job still remained faithful to God, Satan convinced God to let him harm Job physically. Satan covered Job with sores from head to foot, and the poor man scraped himself with a pottery shard to try to get relief. Job was in continual pain emotionally and physically.

"You also look at my scars," Job continues. "That is good. These scars have meaning. There is no pain in them—not in the scars, not in my words, not even in my story any longer. No pain; only promise." Job leans forward. His voice is even and calm, though a bit gravelly when he speaks more quietly.

"People look at my stature, and they often dismiss me. But God gave me the capacity to be bigger on the inside than the outside," he says. "No matter what happens to you—in the worst of circumstances, in your darkest hour, when you have no answers, even when you are suffering greatly, always remember," says Job with calm confidence, "*God sees the big picture.*"

The Promise of the Big Picture

I cannot imagine what Job must have gone through. He lost all his earthly possessions, all ten of his children died, and then his health failed. What a heartbreaking experience. What hard-won wisdom he must possess after surviving all that suffering. When he was in the midst of it, I'm sure he couldn't understand any of it. But from the vantage point of eternity, everything must have finally become clear to him:

1. Satan Did Not See the Big Picture

Job became a target of Satan when God singled the man out for his honesty and integrity, for his devotion to God and avoidance of evil. Satan couldn't bear it. And he believed he could prompt Job to curse God.

But Satan did not see the big picture. He focused on the external. He believed Job was defined by his possessions and his success. If he had been able to see what God saw, he would have seen a man who was defined by his relationship with God rather than his relationship with things. Satan failed to realize that no matter what he did to poor Job, nothing would destroy Job's love for God, nor would he blame God.

Because Satan only saw the blessings that Job received from God, he thought, "Take away the blessings on the outside, and that will change Job inside." But Satan was wrong.

2. Job's Wife Did Not See the Big Picture

When Satan added physical illness to Job's already dire condition, Job scraped the itching sores that covered his entire body, and he waited. Job's wife could not understand his actions. Confronting him as he sat atop an ash heap, she scolded, "Are you still maintaining your integrity? Curse God and die!" Job wouldn't think of it.

Like Satan, Job's wife did not see the big picture. She thought that if Job got rid of God he would get rid of his suffering. But Job was determined to cling to God and accept the bad in life, just as he had accepted the good. He would not curse God.

3. Job's Friends Did Not See the Big Picture

Imagine what it would be like to see one of your best friends, someone highly successful and whom you admired greatly, sitting in a garbage dump, sick, bloody, and grief-stricken. That is what the friends of Job were confronted with when they saw him. They barely recognized him, but they could clearly see his misery. But they, too, could not clearly see the big picture.

Eliphaz, Bildad, Zophar, and Elihu acted superior to Job. They had all the answers. They instructed Job with platitudes, assuming he must have done wrong. They believed the righteous are somehow exempt from suffering, so Job must have sinned greatly. But that's not how life works. No human being has all the answers. And some things cannot be "fixed."

In the end they made Job feel worse, not better. Sometimes the best thing you can do when friends are suffering is simply sit on the ash heap and weep with them.

> *Sometimes the best thing you can do when friends are suffering is simply sit on the ash heap and weep with them.*

4. Job Did Not See the Big Picture

It is ironic that Job was in many ways just as blind as his friends, his wife, and his torturer. He wanted to know, "Why me?" Like us, he wanted to know why bad things happen to good people. In his case, bad things happened in every area of life: home, work, family, friends, possessions, and health. Job's suffering ran the gamut, and was devastating. No wonder his name has become synonymous with suffering.

What seemed like the worst part of all this to Job was that it felt undeserved. As a kid, I did a lot of things that deserved punishment. But the times when I *didn't* do wrong and got punished are the memories that stand out to me. No wonder Job wanted God Himself to tell him why he was suffering. But still he didn't get an answer that he understood. Why? He didn't see the big picture.

5. *God* Did *See the Big Picture*

The good news is that God saw the big picture. He always does. From the very beginning, He saw that Job was bigger and better on the inside than on the outside.

Job was honest inside and out. He was a man of integrity, which means he was whole, and he was consistent through and through. He was able to stay true to God and to himself, no matter what was thrown at him: the destruction of his world, the loss of his possessions, the death of his children, torture at the hands of the Enemy, doubt on the part of his wife, and friends who preached at him instead of empathizing with him.

> *God saw that Job was bigger and better on the inside than on the outside.*

The Bible says that people look at the outside, but God looks at the inside. That is what God did with Job. He saw the big picture because he could see Job on the inside, not just the outside.

- Others saw Job's blessings; God saw Job's inner beauty.

- Others saw Job's love for his family; God saw Job's inner love for Him.
- Others saw Job's fortune; God saw Job's inner faith.

God saw Job more clearly than he saw himself, and God knew him better than he knew himself.

Job's capacity to do right was greater than others expected. His capacity for love was deeper than others hoped. His patience was stronger than others imagined. It's a mark of his capacity on the inside that God asked Job to intercede for his friends, and accepted his prayers in the place of their punishment.

God is bigger than our understanding. He cannot be explained. He will not be questioned. His purpose will be fulfilled. And there will be times when we don't know why. The best we can do is try to be bigger on the inside than the outside and trust that God knows the big picture. Once we understand that, it allows us to rely on Him and trust His ways in our lives.

Life Lessons from Job

We wait as Job readies himself to talk. I can't wait to hear the wisdom that will come from the person whose life has been an example of righteous suffering for thousands of years. Job says...

"Being Bigger on the Inside Than on the Outside Means That Your Character Is Greater Than Your Reputation"

"My reputation before my trials was great. I was a very wealthy man. No one else in my part of the world possessed seven thousand sheep or three thousand camels or five hundred teams of oxen or five hundred donkeys—let alone all of those things. My wealth was beyond my wildest dreams. I needed an army of servants to care for everything. People envied me.

"But those blessings did not define me. Reputation is important, but character is more important. What I put in my heart was my home. My energy and time were spent on growing what was within me: faith, gratitude, patience, love, joy. These things built me from the inside out and became the foundation for my life.

"If you would be great in God's eyes, grow within, not without. Make strong character your greatest goal. It is the only thing you can keep in the darkest of times."

"Being Bigger on the Inside Than on the Outside Means That Your Attitude Is Better Than Your Circumstances"

"Anyone can have a good attitude in the good times. The test is if you can have a good attitude in adversity. Can you remain positive and faithful when circumstances are overwhelming?

"I had no control over my circumstances. You could even say that my circumstances became as negative as they did because I had been so successful. I became a target of the Enemy because I was doing so many things right. But the one thing I always had control of was my attitude. I chose it every morning, in the bad times as well as the good.

"Few people have a good attitude when things are going badly for them. Those few who choose every day to think right even when things are not going right do so even when they don't feel like it. They choose to believe. They choose to rely on God instead of themselves. And those choices make them bigger on the inside."

"Being Bigger on the Inside Than on the Outside Means That Your Faith in God Is Stronger Than Your Vision"

"When everything looked bleak, when everything had been taken from me and there was no indication that anything would get better, I still trusted God. I still believed in Him. That is why I refused to curse Him and die. I could see no hope. I could see no future. I could see no end to my suffering. But I could see God. Every day I would look at the size of my problem and the size of my God. My strength came from knowing that my God was bigger than my problems.

"Be assured, God always has a future planned for us, if not in this world, then in the next. We can depend on Him.

"In my case, God's plan was to give me even more in my second half than He had in my first. He doubled the number of sheep, camels, oxen, and donkeys I possessed. He gave me seven more sons. And my three daughters— oh, my daughters—were unlike any other women in the world. No other women were as beautiful. No other women were as smart. No other women—or men—were more worthy of respect. I gave them the same inheritance as my sons. And God granted me a long and full life. With my own two hands, I got to hold my great-great-great-grandson and bless him.

"God gave me more than I ever hoped or imagined, making me bigger and better on the outside, all because my desire was to be better on the inside. If you want God's best for you, make that your goal."

God gave me more than I ever hoped or imagined, making me bigger and better on the outside, all because my desire was to be better on the inside.

Job's Prayer for Us

As Job begins to stand up, we shift to stand up too. "Don't get up," he says, placing his hands on our arms. "If you stand, I won't be able to reach the tops of your heads as I pray for you." There is a twinkle in his eye—a hint at the edges of his mouth that he's suppressing a smile. There is no self-consciousness in him. He knows who he is and is not trying to impress us.

"Sovereign Lord,

"I ask You to bless these children of Yours as You have blessed me, if not with worldly wealth, then with otherworldly wisdom. Help them to trust

You in the midst of any trial. Give them the peace that passes understanding and assurance that no matter what's happening in their lives, You always see the big picture. Amen."

Leadership Lessons from Job

Job looks from one to the other of us. And then he smiles. It's as if he's telling us, "Don't worry. Everything is going to be all right." He turns and walks unhurriedly away.

We often think of Job as the person who suffered or the rich man who lost it all and gained it back. But he was a leader. He must have had hundreds of servants working for him to care for those thousands of animals and everything that went with them. It would be like running a major corporation today. You don't succeed at that level without leadership. Yet the lessons I think we can learn from him are not in the nuts and bolts of leadership. The lessons come from the inside, from his character:

1. Good Leaders Don't Allow Their Emotions to Dictate Their Decisions

If Job had given in to his emotions, he might have given up. He could have followed the hollow advice of his friends, even though he knew it was wrong, or he could have listened to his wife: he could have cursed God and taken his own life. But he didn't.

Like all good leaders, he did what was right, and then hoped to feel good about it later. He didn't do what felt good and hope it turned out right. When life and leadership get hard, we need to follow Job's example.

2. Good Leaders Know Outside Reputation Should Never Be Greater Than Inside Character

Who people think we are will not sustain us and keep us going when pressures and trials come upon us. Reputation is like a shadow. It has no substance. What will help us to stand up to the press is what we are on the inside. It will determine how we handle the outside.

Only God saw the inside of Job, so He knew Job would be faithful when he was tested. If we want to be faithful too, we need to keep growing on the inside.

3. Good Leaders Realize That Victory Does Not Come Quickly or Easily

It may seem an obvious thing to say, but the best things in life aren't fast, cheap, or easy. We know this intuitively. We know we have to be patient and work hard. Yet somehow we keep forgetting it, and we hope for victory to come at no cost. It just doesn't happen.

When we forget this truth, we should think of Job. His apparent defeat was crushing and looked impossible to overcome, yet in the end he still achieved victory with God as his helper. When we have God, we are always still in the game. That is the big picture.

Job's Discussion Guide

Then Job replied to the Lord:
"I know that you can do all things;
    no purpose of yours can be thwarted.
You asked, 'Who is this that obscures my plans
    without knowledge?'
    Surely I spoke of things I did not understand,
    things too wonderful for me to know.
"You said, 'Listen now, and I will speak;
    I will question you,
    and you shall answer me.'
My ears had heard of you
    but now my eyes have seen you.
Therefore I despise myself
    and repent in dust and ashes." (Job 42:1–6)

1. Do you find it easy or difficult to identify with Job? Why?
2. Have you ever received advice that sounded like it should be right but that your instincts told you was wrong? Explain.
3. In that instance, what did you do? Did you follow the advice or your instincts? How did it turn out?

4. How easy or difficult do you find it to trust God? Explain.
5. What do you think it means to be bigger on the inside than the outside?
6. Where do you believe you need to grow on the inside? Why?
7. What action are you willing to take right away to facilitate that growth?

To learn more about Job, read Job 1:1–42:17 and James 5:11.

JACOB

Let God Have Control of Your Life

The sun outside my window is climbing up the sky. The bright sunlight no longer shines in directly through the windows, but the glare is still bright, its intensity increased by the light reflecting off the ocean. It's after midmorning, and my study is flooded with light.

The person who steps into the doorway of the study is a huge man. He's over six feet tall, with broad shoulders and thick muscular limbs. He looks tough, weather-beaten.

As he moves over toward the chair, we notice that he limps. He drops down into the chair opposite us and puts his huge hands on the arms of the chair. We can see that his hands and thick fingers are callused.

"I have been known by many names: heel catcher, deceiver, father of the tribes. My favorite name is the one God Himself gave me: Israel. The name I received at birth from my father and mother is Jacob.

"Early in my life, all I wanted was to get ahead," says Jacob. "I wanted to control my destiny. And I was willing to do whatever it took to do so. I had my wits, my strong arms, and the will to outwork others. I was always trying to gain an advantage, and I was often able to exploit it. I got the birthright from my brother, Esau, because his stomach was more important to him than his future. And I got the blessing because—well, let's just say that it belonged to me when I received the birthright, and I wanted to make sure it went to its rightful owner.

"I kept trying to make things happen. But I didn't understand God or how He worked. I spent a large part of my life fighting for a future that God had already planned for me. Don't make the same mistake I made," says Jacob. "*Let God have control of your life.*"

Letting Go

I think we all have problems like Jacob's. We don't want to let go of control and let God have it. Richard Foster defines submission as the ability to lay down the terrible burden of needing to get our own way. We, like Jacob, have a tough time with that.

Jacob was always trying to control his world. When

he saw an opportunity to get the birthright from his older twin Esau, Jacob took it. When his mother advised him to trick his father into giving him the blessing because Isaac thought he was Esau, Jacob took advantage of it. And when his brother Esau got angry, Jacob fled to his uncle Laban's house.

Like Jacob we resist God. And often it takes a crisis in our lives to get us to change. That was certainly the case for Jacob. He went through a process to become dependent on God. I think that for us to experience the same growth, we need to experience a similar pattern:

1. We Run Out of Options

After twenty years working for his father-in-law Laban, Jacob recognized that he had worn out his welcome. Staying was not an option, because Laban and his sons had become hostile toward him. So Jacob packed up his family and livestock, and he fled.

That solution created another problem: Jacob had to face Esau. Now Jacob would be stuck between a rock and a hard place. He was out of options. He sent Esau gifts. He called him master. And he divided his family into different traveling groups, hoping at least some of them might survive if Esau attacked. But in the end, no matter what, he had to face his brother when he set out for home.

Mother Teresa said, "You will never know God is all you need until He is all you have." God knows that when we run out of options, we are finally ready to turn to Him. We often see such circumstances as a crisis. God sees them as an opportunity to help us.

> "You will never know God is all you need until He is all you have."
> —Mother Teresa

2. We Face God Alone

When Jacob was alone and had nowhere to turn, he finally faced God. And he wrestled with Him. This is what we often do. We look to God when we need something, when we have a question we can't answer, when we're afraid, or when we don't know what to do. We ask God to be on our agenda. But that's not going to happen. God cares for us, and He wants to meet our needs, but He will never be on our agenda. If we face God, we realize that.

Randy Alcorn wrote, "To me brokenness is more than just periodic times of intense emotional experience; it's an ongoing sense of inadequacy. When I come to a point, as I face life's difficulties, where I know I can't just fix things, including myself, it's a much-needed reminder that

He's the Vine, I'm a branch, and apart from Him I can do nothing."[1] We have to come to God on His terms.

3. We Lose Ourselves

Even as Jacob wrestled with God, he still tried to stay in control. He refused to let go of his opponent. And he insisted on receiving a blessing. He still hoped to dictate terms, just as he had the first time he encountered God at Bethel. Back then, Jacob wanted God to be with him, watch over him, give him food, provide him with clothes, and return him to his father's house before he was willing to submit to Him.[2] This time at Peniel, Jacob was not in control. If he wanted to be blessed by God, he had to submit to God.

That is the way God works. If we want to gain His favor, we must be willing to lose ourselves. We must lose our life to save it.[3] We must allow God to lead us. As C. S. Lewis said, "I become my own only when I give myself to Another." We must give ourselves to God.

> "I become my own only when I give myself to Another."
> —C. S. Lewis

Too often we are like a horse who allows his master to put a bit in his mouth, but then fights against it. What we don't seem to understand is that if we allow God to have complete control of the reins in our life, He will stay with us continually, and He will guide us away from danger, see that we are fed, and lead us back home—the very things Jacob longed for.

4. God Breaks Us in the Right Places

Before Jacob ever wrestled with God, he was a broken person. He was deceptive, impatient, and manipulative. He had sacrificed relationships with the most important people in his life to get ahead. But God broke him in a different way. He used the pain of dislocating Jacob's hip to get his attention. When Jacob felt that pain, he no longer was focused on winning. He became focused on God's blessing. He realized that receiving the guidance and favor of God was more important than anything else. And Jacob's God-directed brokenness would open the door for the healing of those other kinds of brokenness.

> *We don't need to be fixed to come to God. We need to be broken.*

We don't need to be fixed to come to God. We need to be broken. When we stop striving and start listening, when we slow down enough for God to get our attention, then He can help us. He can put us back together again. He can help us to become who He created us to be.

5. We Finally Find Ourselves

When God asked Jacob, "What is your name?" it wasn't because He didn't know it. He asked Jacob his name because He wanted Jacob to admit who he was. The name Jacob means "heel catcher" or "deceiver." God wanted Jacob to admit what he was so he could become what he could be. Jacob—the trickster, the mama's boy who deceived his brother, the liar who fooled his father— would be changed into a new person—the servant, the humble parent who would try to guide his children, the father of a nation. God gave him a new name: Israel, which means "he struggles with God."

What a great name that is! It could apply to you and me because, after all, who doesn't struggle with God? I think we all have a hard time letting God be in charge of our lives. But, like Jacob, we need to surrender our old selves to become our new, better selves.

Life Lessons from Jacob

I cannot wait to hear what someone who wrestled with God has to say. We don't have to wait long. He immediately starts speaking:

"Brokenness Precedes a Breakthrough"

"The first third of my life I spent trying to make a breakthrough. I wanted to be successful. I wanted to have influence. I wanted to be someone important. But I could not achieve any of these things until I became broken and humble before God.

"The more self-reliant and self-absorbed I was, the more difficult it was for God to get my attention. God tried to speak to me in a gentle way at Bethel. He showed me a vision. But I was hardheaded. I wanted to prove myself. I had my own ideas about what I should be doing with my life. If God was willing to help me on my terms, I was open to that. But I wasn't going to go out of my way," says Jacob. "It wasn't until God broke me and hurt my hip that I really understood Who God was—the Almighty God, not just the God of my fathers.

"Don't make God do things the hard way with you. When He's trying to communicate with you, listen to His quiet voice. Don't go your own way. Submit to Him and allow Him to break you gently. We cannot be of much use to God until we are broken. We must be humble before God and let Him take control of our lives. I was able to do that when I realized God is always right."

"You Must Lose Yourself to Find Yourself"

"My goal in life was to become wealthy and have a large family," says Jacob. "I fought to achieve that goal. I worked seven years to have Rachel as my wife. When Laban tricked me and substituted Leah in her place on our wedding day, I worked another seven years to earn Rachel. God gave me the large family I desired. And He gave me wealth too. But God's goal for me was so much bigger than my own. He wanted me to father a nation! He wanted the children of my offspring to be kings. He wanted my family to bring forth the Messiah!

"For God to use me, I had to give up my nature, let go of my pride, set aside my agenda, and lose the identity I'd built all my life. I had to give up being Jacob. I had to let God redefine me. My willingness to obey God had to become more important than my identity.

"Don't allow what you *think* you want to get in the way of who God *knows* you can be. Let go of your agenda. Hand your goals over to God. Give Him control," Jacob says. "It's never too late to let God lead you to a better life, the way a shepherd leads a favorite sheep to better pastures."

"When You Find Yourself on God's Terms, You Find Fulfillment"

"The ultimate goal in life is to find your purpose and then lose yourself in living it. In a sense, you lose yourself twice. First you lose your old self—the prideful, willful one—by letting God have control of your life. Then you lose yourself in devotion to fulfilling that purpose. That's where the true fulfillment comes in life. You understand why God put you here, what your gifts are, how you can best serve Him. You know your *why*.

"Do you want what you hope might be good for you? Or do you want the very best? God created you, just as He created me," says Jacob. "God knows who you are—not who you hope to be, not who you wish you were, not who your parents wanted you to become, or who someone else expects you to be—but who you *really* are. And He has a plan for your life. If you let God have control of your life, you will experience it."

Jacob's Prayer for Us

"*O God my Lord and Master,*

"*I ask for the blessing that only You can give on these children of Yours. Help them to*

see themselves as You see them. As they let go
of their old selves by giving You control of their
lives, show them why You created them, and guide
them in the path You have prepared for them. In
Your kind and compassionate name. Amen."

Leadership Lessons from Jacob

We gratefully accept Jacob's blessing. His words ring true.
I know that every time I have allowed God to have control
of an area of my life, I have experienced fulfillment. I'd
bet that has also been true for you.

What can we learn from Jacob's journey?

1. Lordship Precedes Godly Leadership

I think that many of us are like Jacob. We are inclined
to allow God only conditional access to our lives. We
give Him a list of conditions He must first meet for us
to follow Him. Or perhaps we start our relationship with

Him with exceptional gratitude, but we really only let
Him have control in the one
or two areas that have been
the greatest sources of pain
or frustration. At that point

> *We cannot be what God*
> *intends us to be and*
> *at the same time hold*
> *on to who we think we*
> *should be.*

we feel it's enough. But that is a mistake. We cannot be what God intends us to be and at the same time hold on to who we think we should be. That was Jacob's mistake for too long.

I'm reminded of the words of C. S. Lewis, who wrote,

Imagine yourself as a living house. God comes in to rebuild that house. At first, perhaps you can understand what He is doing. He is getting the drains right and stopping the leaks in the roof and so on: you know that those jobs needed doing and so you are not surprised. But presently He starts knocking the house about in a way that hurts abominably and does not seem to make sense. What on earth is He up to? The explanation is that He is building quite a different house from the one you thought of—throwing out a new wing here, putting on an extra floor there, running up towers, making courtyards. You thought you were going to be made into a decent little cottage: but He is building a palace. He intends to come and live in it Himself![4]

God does not want *a* place in our lives. He wants the first place. His throne is not a duplex! If we are to be useful to God as leaders, we need to allow Him to rebuild us first. That means allowing Him to use the sledgehammer to knock some things down that need to go, and letting Him use the carpenter's hammer to build some things we lack.

2. Being in Control Limits Our Leadership

People often mistakenly believe they will get more out of life if they try to control it, when in fact the opposite is true. People who try to keep control usually gravitate to others like themselves. Jacob, who was a deceiver, ended up working for Laban, who kept trying to cheat him. He also fell in love with Rachel, who stole her father's household goods and lied to cover it up.

People who try to stay in control also end up hurting the people they love to get what they want. Jacob's father Isaac was crushed when he realized that he had given his blessing to Jacob instead of Esau. And Esau was ready to kill his twin brother because of what had happened. It required a twenty-year cooling-off period plus the intervention of God for the brothers to make peace with one another.

Worst of all, people who try to take control of their own lives live far beneath their privileges. It was clear from before the time Jacob was born that he would be a leader of significance. Here's why:

- God gave his mother Rebekah a prophecy say-ing that Jacob would father a nation and his older brother would serve him.[5]
- Jacob possessed the birthright after receiving it in trade from his brother.
- Jacob received his father Isaac's blessing.
- God came to Jacob in a vision and promised to give him the land, be with him, watch over him, and bless all the people of the earth through him.

What more proof did he need?

Jacob's future was secure. God had a plan for him, yet Jacob lived as though his future were uncertain. He occupied his time with fighting for a future that belonged to him all along.

The same kind of thing can happen with us. If God is for us, who can be against us? If we give God control of our lives, we should live and lead as though we really believe it. And we can rest assured: God takes complete responsibility for the life that is given completely to Him.

> *God takes complete responsibility for the life that is given completely to Him.*

Jacob's Discussion Guide

So Jacob was left alone, and a man wrestled with him till daybreak. When the man saw that he could not overpower him, he touched the socket of Jacob's hip so that his hip was wrenched as he wrestled with the man. Then the man said, "Let me go, for it is daybreak."

But Jacob replied, "I will not let you go unless you bless me."

The man asked him, "What is your name?"

"Jacob," he answered.

Then the man said, "Your name will no longer be Jacob, but Israel, because you have struggled with God and with humans and have overcome."

Jacob said, "Please tell me your name."

But he replied, "Why do you ask my name?" Then he blessed him there.

So Jacob called the place Peniel, saying, "It is because I saw God face to face, and yet my life was spared." (Genesis 32:24–30)

1. Since there was a prophecy about Jacob and how he would rule over his brother, do you think Jacob needed to exploit his brother during a weak moment

and deceive his father into giving him the blessing? Explain.

2. When you feel like you're at a dead end or have run out of options, how do you usually respond?

3. Jacob wrestled with God face-to-face. Have you ever experienced a time when you felt like you were wrestling with God? What was the outcome?

4. Have you ever felt like you were broken and rebuilt by God in an area? What was that like?

5. Jacob lived beneath his privileges because he kept fighting for himself and trying to promote himself. What privileges do you think you might be forgoing because you're not allowing God into areas of your life?

6. How difficult do you find it to release control of your life to God? Explain.

7. Where is God currently asking you to let go?

8. What step can you take now to allow God greater access to your life?

To learn more about Jacob, read Genesis 25:19–34, 27:1–35:29, 37:1–36, 42:1–2, 42:36–38, 46:1–30, and 48:3–50:14.

DEBORAH

God Specializes in the Unexpected

We hear faint footsteps on the floor in the hallway coming our way. The next moment, a figure stands in the doorway of the study. She could not be a greater contrast to Jacob. He was a hulking man. This is a woman—a rather small woman—but with an air of command. She wastes no time moving across the room and settles easily into the chair.

"In my time, the people of Israel did evil, so God gave us over to a king of Canaan who oppressed us. A few people, like me, pleaded with God to deliver us, and finally after twenty years He heard our cries. It was to me that He gave instructions for what we should do. I am Deborah. And there is something you need to know," she says. *"God specializes in the unexpected."*

With God, Expect the Unexpected

It's Deborah, one of the judges who ruled the Hebrews after Joshua died and before God allowed the people to have a king.

"The account of God's interaction with people," says Deborah, "is one story after another of God doing the unexpected. Time after time God showed His people that He doesn't think the way they think, and He doesn't work the way they work."

> *God's interaction with people is one story after another of God doing the unexpected.*

How true. Person after person in Scripture was surprised by God:

- Noah was surprised when God told him He would save him and his family while destroying the earth with a flood.
- Abraham was surprised when God said he would be father of a nation when he had no child.
- Joseph's brothers were surprised when the brother they'd sold as a slave ended up the leader of Egypt.
- Moses was surprised when God wanted a meek stutterer to lead the Israelites.

- Samuel was surprised when God told him David would be the next king.
- David surprised everyone when God gave him Goliath's head in personal combat.
- Naaman was surprised when he was asked to bathe in the Jordan River and God healed him.

And the list goes on. God likes to surprise us. Even Deborah's story is a fantastic illustration of how God does the unexpected:

1. She Was an Unexpected Leader

At a time when women had few rights and the rulers, warriors, and decision-makers of the world were men, Deborah was the judge of Israel. She held court, and Israelites from all over the country came to her so she could settle disputes, much as the children of Israel had sought out Moses when they were in the desert.

But Deborah was also more than a judge. She was a prophet—unlike all the other judges of the Old Testament. Most of the other judges were warriors, and when God spoke to them, He did so through angels. But God delivered His messages directly to Deborah, which was very uncommon. The Bible has record of only eight prophets before Deborah.

Deborah was an unusual and exceptional leader at a time when women normally were unable to rise up. But God raised her up, showing that He enjoys using people others might discount or dismiss.

2. *She Delivered an Unexpected Message*

After the Israelites experienced twenty years of oppression, Deborah received a message from God that He wanted to help them. And God was very specific. He wanted Barak to command ten companies of soldiers and make them ready to do battle in the Kishon River valley. God would deliver the Canaanite king's army and Sisera, the commander, there.

The question was how the Israelites would respond. After all, their expectations for themselves were low. They had been oppressed for a generation and had done nothing to free themselves.

The expectations of the Canaanites regarding them were also low. On their own, the Israelites would have had no chance to win a battle. The Canaanites who ruled over them were well armed and equipped with nine hundred iron chariots—the equivalent of tanks against poorly trained foot soldiers today.

But God had different expectations for them. With His help, He knew they would win.

Deborah shared God's confidence, so she may have been surprised when she delivered the message from God to Barak and he refused to go on his mission without her. Maybe he believed they could not win without her presence, that she needed to watch the battle the way Moses had watched and prayed as Joshua fought the Amalekites. Maybe he wanted her to die along with him if their forces were defeated. Who knows? But she agreed to go. So we can add military commander to her list of unexpected titles, along with judge and prophet.

3. God Intervened in an Unexpected Way

Warren W. Wiersbe said, "If you can explain what God is doing in your ministry, then God is not really in it." God wants us to wait and depend on Him. He delights in showing His creativity. Scripture is filled with stories of unusual and unexpected ways that God defeated enemies on behalf of His people. He used plagues, confusion in the camp to have people kill one another, tumors, and earthquakes. In this case it was water. A flash flood changed the valley, which would normally have been an excellent staging area

> *"If you can explain what God is doing in your ministry, then God is not really in it."*
> —*Warren W. Wiersbe*

for a battle using chariots, into a bog. Stuck in the soft ground, the chariots became useless, and the Israelites defeated the enemy army.

The great irony in this was that Baal, the main god of the Canaanite forces, was supposed to be ruler of storms and weather. Yet the Canaanites lost the battle because of a storm!

We should never ask or expect God to dumb down His extraordinary plans to fit into our tiny minds. Why should we expect God to be restricted by our limited understanding?

4. The Result Was an Unexpected Victory

To the people who finally believed in God and obeyed Him, the victory was expected. But to the rest of the world it must have been a surprise. So was the way Sisera, the enemy commander, was killed. As Sisera's army was being defeated, he ran away. When he arrived at the tent of a supposed ally, he thought he was safe. But when he fell asleep, a woman named Jael drove a tent peg through his skull and killed him. As a result, Israel's victory was complete.

Life Lessons from Deborah

Deborah is a tremendous example of a leader who had influence in spiritual life, community affairs, government, and the military. I feel certain she has a lot to teach us.

"Be Willing to Stand Out When Others Don't Expect It"

"When I summoned Barak and told him that God commanded that he fight the Canaanite army, the people could understand his hesitation. We had been under the thumb of King Jabin for twenty years. Everyone was afraid of him," says Deborah. "What they did not expect was for me to say yes when Barak asked me to accompany him into battle. No one in Israel had ever seen such a thing.

"God wants to use unexpected people, like you and me. He wants men and women who are willing to stand out and go against the grain. What others think doesn't matter. Only God's view of your potential does. You don't have to live under

> *God wants to use unexpected people, like you and me.*

people's limitations, because you serve a God Who is limitless.

"You and I are bigger than the way the world sees

us. There is more in you than what your parents, friends, teachers, fellow laborers, or leaders see in you. Don't take on limitations that don't belong to you. No matter how others view you, God can use you. He is waiting and ready to give you a chance to make a difference. You are already on His list of recipients of the unexpected, like Noah, Abraham, and the rest. God wants to surprise the world through you."

> *You are already on His list of recipients of the unexpected, like Noah, Abraham, and the rest. God wants to surprise the world through you.*

"Be Willing to Speak Out When God Expects It"

"The people of Israel came to me to judge their disputes. They were used to hearing my voice and respected my wisdom. But it was another matter for me to ask them to rise up and fight against our enemies. I was not sure how they would react," says Deborah. "But I could not let my doubt or their fear keep me from fulfilling God's will and speaking up.

"God promised He would provide an army from the tribes of Naphtali and Zebulun. He promised to lure Sisera into the Kishon River valley. He promised to give us victory. I do not doubt God's promises. They are as solid as bedrock," says Deborah.

"You cannot be God's servant and do what He asks only when you feel like it or when it is safe. Serving God is not always safe. Speaking out for Him is not always safe. But while there may not always be safety in standing up and speaking out *for* God, there is always security *in* God."

> *While there may not always be safety in standing up and speaking out for God, there is always security in God.*

"Be Willing to Step Out When Others Depend on It"

"Was it my responsibility to go to battle? Did God ask me to lead the army? No," Deborah explains. "That was Barak's responsibility. It was God's command that Barak march out and defeat Sisera. But God's people were depending on us to obey Him and bring the victory. If we as leaders are not willing to step out, then we let our people down. They cannot follow where we do not lead.

"So I went to war for God and my people. It was uncomfortable. It was unexpected. It was right. And God fulfilled His promise, as I'd known He would. And He gave the honor of stopping Sisera's abuse of the people to another woman. Praise God.

"If you are a leader," Deborah says, "you must step out when your people are depending on you. Your courage is their courage. Your obedience is their obedience. Your victory is their victory. Don't let it slip away."

Deborah's Prayer for Us

"O Mighty God of Israel,

"Teach my friends to always have the courage to break new ground for You. Grant them wisdom. Make them bold. Give them the confidence that comes only from You. And give them victory! Amen."

Leadership Lessons from Deborah

With that, she is done. She stands up and, without looking at either one of us, she walks away. I am struck by the confidence and wisdom of this leader and giant of the faith. We can see that she would easily command any room she entered. No wonder Barak wanted her with him when he went into battle.

Pastor Jack Hayford observed, "Nothing is more limiting than the self-imposed boundaries we clamp around our own lives when we require God to fit into our expectations." Deborah certainly did not do that. She was open to what God wanted to do. Her story makes it clear that God wants to connect with us by coming down to where we are, but His desire is to raise us up to where we could be.

There are many leadership lessons we can learn from Deborah:

1. When One Leader Refuses, God Often Asks Another to Take His Place

When leaders aren't doing their jobs, God often invites other leaders to take their place. When Barak refused, God raised up Deborah. Had she refused, someone else would have taken her place. God's will can be fulfilled through leaders. And reluctant leaders may be given the chance for a change of heart and therefore a second chance to lead. But God's will cannot be thwarted by leaders. God is sovereign. So the question becomes, who will lead?

When God asks us to do something for Him as a leader, it's a privilege. It's an invitation, not an obligation. Will we accept it? If we allow fear to stop us, as Barak did, then the blessing will go to someone else, as it did to Jael. Don't miss it.

2. We Should Not Put Limitations on Leaders When God Doesn't

In their day, Deborah and Jael would have been dismissed by most people. Women had few rights, and they were not expected to lead. But Deborah and Jael didn't allow others to limit them. They allowed themselves what Bob Pierce of World Vision calls "God room." They did what they could, seizing the opportunities God gave them, knowing there was a gap between what they were doing and what needed to happen. God had to fill that gap.

We need to be more like them. We need to forget what others think of us, let go of our past, and do everything in our power to reach our potential as leaders—and then expect God to do what only He can do. And we need to treat other potential leaders the same way, expecting God to help them if they ask Him to.

What might God do with you or me if we didn't put limitations on ourselves? What people might we be able to serve? What victories might we be able to win with God's help? The possibilities are as great as God is.

3. When Godly Leaders Obey God's Call, the People Are Blessed

Whenever leaders rise up and fulfill their calling, the people they serve are blessed. In the case of Deborah, the people threw off the yoke of oppression and enjoyed peace for forty years. That was a fantastic legacy Deborah gave the Israelites because she was willing to let God do the unexpected with her.

If you are a leader and you want your people to be blessed, be an example to them and obey God's call on your life. Follow Him with integrity wherever He leads. And don't be afraid to let others get the credit. God is mighty, and there is plenty of His blessing to go around for everyone.

Deborah's Discussion Guide

Now Deborah, a prophet, the wife of Lappidoth, was leading Israel at that time. She held court under the Palm of Deborah between Ramah and Bethel in the hill country of Ephraim, and the Israelites went up to her to have their disputes decided. She sent for Barak son of Abinoam from Kedesh in Naphtali and said to him, "The Lord, the God of Israel, commands you: 'Go, take with you ten thousand men of Naphtali and Zebulun and lead them up to Mount Tabor. I will lead Sisera, the commander of Jabin's army, with his chariots and his troops to the Kishon River and give him into your hands.'"

Barak said to her, "If you go with me, I will go; but if you don't go with me, I won't go."

"Certainly I will go with you," said Deborah. "But because of the course you are taking, the honor will not be yours, for the Lord will deliver Sisera into the hands of a woman." So Deborah went with Barak to Kedesh. There Barak summoned Zebulun and Naphtali, and ten thousand men went up under his command. Deborah also went up with him. (Judges 4:4–10)

1. How do you imagine Deborah came to be a judge in that period of Israel's history?
2. Has God ever done something unexpected for you? What was it, and how did you respond?
3. Do you find it difficult or easy to speak out for God? Why?
4. What kinds of limitations do you believe other people have put on you? How have you dealt with them?
5. What do you think you might be able to do for God if you were able to throw off those limitations and trust Him to surprise you?
6. What would you need to do or what help would you require to throw off those limitations? Are you willing to take those steps today?
7. Might God be asking you to step up to lead? If so, would you be willing to do it?

To learn more about Deborah, read Judges 4:1–5:31.

ISAIAH

*God Has a Reason for Your
Encounter with Him*

It is early afternoon, and we are still thinking about the words of Deborah when we hear the footsteps of the next person coming down the hallway. When he turns the corner, we see he is tall and thin, wearing pale-blue clothing. His eyes are intelligent and he somehow reminds us of a professor. Over his shoulder is slung a cloth bag filled with lumpy cylindrical objects. Out of the top of the bag peeks the end of one of them, and I realize it's a scroll.

When the man sits down and places his hands in his lap, we can see that the tip of the thumb and first two fingers of his right hand are stained black.

That's ink, I think to myself. He must be a writer, but who? He could be any of the more than a dozen giants of the faith whose writing became part of the Bible. Which one is he?

"I grew up with a love for words, and I enjoyed expressing myself in verse. But to be brutally honest, what I wrote in my early years was juvenile and trite," he says. "Then I had an encounter with the Living God, and everything changed. From then on, I was a poet—and more than a poet. I was a prophet of the Most High God."

He looks at me and then you, an inquiring expression on his face. "You still do not know who I am, do you? I am Isaiah," he says, as he cracks a smile. "Mark my words," he says, his expression changing. *"God has a reason for your encounter with Him."*

God Is on the Throne

Of course. Isaiah, the man who has been called the prince of prophets and the Shakespeare of the Bible. Not only was he a poet and prophet, but he was also a great preacher. I know we can learn a lot from him.

1. Our Greatest Loss Can Be a Catalyst for Our Greatest Gain

When King Uzziah died, Isaiah and the rest of God's people must have been shaken. For fifty-two years the same king had reigned. For fifty years they had experienced security. Scripture says Uzziah had done what was right in the eyes of God, so his was a good reign over Judah. With life expectancy being as short as it was in the ancient world, that meant most people in the nation had known no king other than Uzziah. So the question troubling everyone was, who would sit on the throne?

It was in this context that Isaiah received the vision of God on His throne. Judah's loss was Isaiah's gain. He might have lost his earthly king, but he saw God Who rules over the entire universe on His throne, His train filling the room, and heavenly beings, the seraphim, crying out to one another,

> Holy, holy, holy is the Lord Almighty;
> The whole earth is full of His glory![6]

That often seems to be the way God works. He uses our losses, failures, and challenges to get our attention, so that He can show Himself to us, grow us, and draw us nearer to Him.

2. *When We See God, We See Ourselves*

When Isaiah saw the heavenly throne room with God Himself high and exalted, spied the six-winged seraphim who covered their eyes in the presence of God, and heard their voices that shook him the way an earthquake would, what was his reaction? He realized his own sinfulness and inadequacy.

> "Woe to me!" I cried. "I am ruined! For I am a man of unclean lips, and I live among a people of unclean lips, and my eyes have seen the King, the Lord Almighty."[7]

When we encounter God and get a sense of His holiness and purity and power and glory, we cannot help but be humbled. It prompts us to confess our sins, which is really just humility in action.

My friend Andy Stanley says that someone once said to him, "I would like God to talk directly to me." Andy's response was, "No you wouldn't. If God talked directly to you, He would not be telling you what you want to hear."

3. An Encounter with God Inspires Us to Serve Him

Isaiah's first reaction to God was awe, because of God's glory. His second was fear, because of his inadequacy. But his third response was a desire to serve. When God asked, "Whom shall I send? And who will go for us?" Isaiah said, "Here am I. Send me!"[8]

When we truly encounter God and get a sense of His

love for us, despite all our shortcomings, how can we feel anything other than gratitude? And how can we better show our gratitude than by serving Him?

Life Lessons from Isaiah

Out of this experience with God, Isaiah wanted to go to the people with His message. But he could not have taken the life-changing message to others without first encountering the life-changing God. This is how God works in our lives. An encounter with God is a prerequisite for His sending us out to be a messenger for Him. We must be changed before we can encourage others to change.

As we think about this truth, the changed messenger before us begins to speak:

"God Wants to Reveal Himself to You"

"For centuries people have been amazed by the vision God gave me of Himself while I was still on earth. What many people don't realize is that God wants to reveal Himself to *everyone*. He wants to reveal Himself to you.

"When I wrote the account of my encounter with God," Isaiah continues, "it was no accident that I used

Lord, the personal name of God, to describe Him, not *Adonai*, which emphasizes God's sovereignty, holiness, and power. Yes, God is sovereign. Yes, God is holy. Yes, God is powerful. But God is also personal.

"God desires to connect with you. He may not do it through a vision as He did for me. I didn't choose the way God revealed Himself to me. Nor would I have asked for it to be that way. But it was perfect for me, and now I realize no other way could have been better.

"Let go of your preconceived notions. Stop trying to dictate how God should show Himself. Be open to whatever He has for you."

"God Wants to Change You"

"When I got a clear picture of God, I got a deep sense of my own sin," Isaiah says. "My response was immediate and clear. Woe to me!" Isaiah says, his voice cracking and tears filling his eyes. "What I discovered that day was that until I became nothing, God could make nothing out of me. Humility overcame me because I saw my true self before God and heard His calling on my life.

"If a person does not humble himself, he leaves God no choice but to humble him. God is God, and there is no other. Before my encounter, I was wrapped up in myself.

God does not allow His work to be thwarted by someone like that.

"Just as God provided for my sin by sending a seraph to touch me with a hot coal and cleanse me, God will cleanse you if you allow Him to. God wants us to feel the weight of our unworthiness, but He never wants to leave us there. Confess your inadequacy and ask God to cleanse you. He will. And then you will begin to change for the better, one step at a time. You cannot get to your future until you settle your past.

> *God loves you, even as you are, but He does not want to leave you where you are.*

"God loves you, even as you are, but He does not want to leave you where you are. He wants to help you change for the better. That is His nature. If you allow Him to, He will help you change little by little, day by day. He never wants to see us stop growing. And with His help, we never will stop."

"God Wants to Use You"

"If you know the story of God's people, you know that over and over again, God reveals Himself to people, changes them, and then gives them assignments," says Isaiah. "That was true for me. When I saw God and was cleansed, He asked who would go for Him. And I quickly responded, 'Here am I! Send me.' I felt privileged to serve God.

"I want you to notice something. God did not compel me to go. He did not command me to go. He *allowed* me to go. I accepted God's invitation, and I was overjoyed when He told me to go and tell my people what He had to say.

"The same can be true for you," says Isaiah. "God has an assignment for you. He won't force you to take it. He will offer it to you, and you must choose it freely. You must volunteer. When He calls you to it, you won't feel worthy. But if you say yes, it will be the best part of life for you. When you are doing what God asks you to do, you know why you exist, why you are breathing air. God always has a reason in mind when we encounter Him. The encounter is personal, and so is the assignment.

"I can't tell you what God will invite you to do. Only God can do that," Isaiah concludes. "But I will tell you this: it will probably be in the area where God has affected you most deeply. God often allows us to help others in the places where He has helped us the most. Where God touches you, He will use you to touch others."

> *Where God touches you, He will use you to touch others.*

Isaiah's Prayer for Us

"O Holy One of Israel,

"I ask that You give these friends a life-changing encounter with You. Call them by name. Touch them. Draw them near to You. And give them assignments that will bring them joy, others healing, and You glory. In Your most powerful and holy name. Amen."

Leadership Lessons from Isaiah

As Isaiah finishes speaking, I realize that he has asked God to give us what we most desire: His touch. If we experience an encounter with God even once, we long for it again for the rest of our lives. We can never experience God's presence too much. It makes us long for heaven.

Isaiah was an influencer during his lifetime, and he has continued to influence people ever since through the Word of God. What leadership lessons can we learn from him?

1. When There Is a Crisis—God Prepares a Leader

King Uzziah was leading God's people well. Though he did make the mistake of trying to offer God incense in the temple when he wasn't supposed to and this caused him to be afflicted with leprosy, he honored God and led people in the right direction. But then he died. That didn't take God by surprise. God didn't say, "Oh no. My leader died. What now?" No, God did what He always does: He raised up another leader. He put Isaiah in place to influence the next three kings: Jotham, Ahaz, and Hezekiah.

2. God Always Calls the Leaders He Prepares

When there is a crisis, God always prepares new leaders and He always invites them to lead. The question is whether they will answer the call. Not all do, as Isaiah did. But they always get the opportunity. The greatest leaders all have this in common: they rise up to meet the anxiety and fear of the people and lead them forward through it.

Be attentive to what God may be calling you to do. If you are frustrated, discouraged, or distraught by the situation you are in, and no one seems to be leading, God might be preparing you for the task. If He invites you to step forward, don't be afraid to respond to His call. It just may lead you to do the thing God created you for.

3. Leaders Need a Touch of God Before They Go Touch the People

Isaiah began his leadership with a touch from God. It was his starting point. But he no doubt needed to continue looking to God and receiving His touch in order to lead and serve others. And it's clear that Isaiah stayed in touch with God. Isaiah once spoke to King Hezekiah, telling him God said the king would die. Isaiah then started to walk away. But the king repented, and before Isaiah was even able to leave the building, God told him to turn around and say that He would heal the king.[9] Clearly Isaiah stayed connected to God all the time.

If you are a leader, seek God before any undertaking. Don't try to touch the people until you've received a touch from God. He will guide and direct you, and He will give you strength and favor to lead for Him.

Isaiah's Discussion Guide

In the year that King Uzziah died, I saw the Lord, high and exalted, seated on a throne; and the train of his robe filled the temple. Above him were seraphim, each with six wings: With two wings they covered their faces, with two they covered their feet, and with two they were flying. And they were calling to one another:

"Holy, holy, holy is the Lord Almighty;

the whole earth is full of his glory."

At the sound of their voices the doorposts and thresholds shook and the temple was filled with smoke.

"Woe to me!" I cried. "I am ruined! For I am a man of unclean lips, and I live among a people of unclean lips, and my eyes have seen the King, the Lord Almighty."

Then one of the seraphim flew to me with a live coal in his hand, which he had taken with tongs from the altar. With it he touched my mouth and said, "See, this has touched your lips; your guilt is taken away and your sin atoned for."

Then I heard the voice of the Lord saying, "Whom shall I send? And who will go for us?"

And I said, "Here am I. Send me!" (Isaiah 6:1–8)

1. In the book of Isaiah, the prophet uses different names of God, sometimes indicating God's power and holiness, and at other times His personal nature. Which of those approaches do you feel most comfortable with? Why?

2. Have you ever experienced a loss or tragedy that acted as a catalyst for change in your life? Explain. Did you invite God into the process?

3. Do you believe that God *wants* to reveal Himself to you? Explain.

4. Have you ever had an experience like Isaiah's in which you felt God was connecting with you personally? Explain.

5. If you have not ever felt connected to God, what do you think it would take for you to be able to experience it?

6. Do you have a sense of how God desires to use you for His glory? If so, describe it.

7. Is God currently asking you to take a specific step or do a particular task? If so, what is it, and will you do it? If not, are you open to hearing from Him?

To learn more about Isaiah, read 2 Kings 19:1–20:21, 2 Chronicles 26:1–23 and 32:1–33, and Isaiah 1:1–66:24.

JONAH

God Always Gives Us a Second Chance

I start to reflect on whom we've already met: a prophet who became discouraged after performing one of the Old Testament's greatest miracles, the mild-mannered servant who succeeded him and did twice as many miracles as his mentor, the righteous man who went to hell on earth and back again to glorify God, a deceiver who gave God control of his life, a woman who judged Israel and expected the unexpected, and a prophetic poet who saw God and lived to tell about it. I try to imagine who might be next.

When we get a look at the person who walks into my study, we're shocked. I've never seen anyone like him before. He looks—I can think of no other word to describe him—*colorless*. His clothes are faded and worn out. They're not really white, but I'm not sure what color they once were.

The man's skin is nearly the same color as his clothes, almost like it has been bleached. And his skin is an odd texture. It reminds me of how people's fingertips look when they've been in a bathtub too long.

As he gets closer and sits down, I realize he is bald, not just on top but completely, like someone who shaves his head. But given the finely wrinkled texture of his skin, even on his scalp, I find it hard to believe he could use a razor on his head. Then I realize. He has no eyebrows either. Or eyelashes. I scan his arms. There is no hair there either. What an odd-looking man.

He sits looking at us without saying a word. Finally I ask, "Who are you?"

"God asked me to go east," the man says. "I chose to go west. He told me to go by land; I chose to go by sea. He asked me to live for others; I made choices for only myself. He asked me to go to Nineveh; I set out for Tarshish. God asked me to rise up and speak for Him; instead I tried to hide.

"I thought I knew better than God," he says, "but of course I didn't. My name is Jonah, and I'm here to tell you: *God always gives us a second chance.*"

The Kindness and Mercy of God

A second chance! What a wonderful message. Jonah's statement to us reminds me of twelve of the most amazing words contained in all of Scripture: "Then the word of the Lord came to Jonah a second time."

After all that Jonah had done, God offered him another opportunity. That's something that should give each of us hope.

1. God Gives Us a Second Chance Because We Need It

When Jonah was called to preach to the people of Nineveh, he tried to get away from God and his calling by jumping aboard a ship and heading for Tarshish. That was two thousand miles away from Nineveh! But when the storm came and threatened to sink the ship, Jonah knew it was his fault. In order to save the others on board, he asked them to cast him into the sea.

Jonah appeared to be doomed, but he cried out to God. And God gave him a second chance. He saved Jonah by providing a great fish to swallow him. That must be why Jonah's skin looks the way it does. He spent three days inside the animal.

There isn't a human being who's ever lived who didn't need a do-over. If you want to see the longest list of mess-ups, don't look in the mirror; look in the Bible. It reveals the mistakes people make and their need for God's grace: Moses committed murder and ran away. Gideon hid in a winepress while his nation was being plundered, and later set up an idol on the very spot where he had received his call from God. Sarah laughed at God's promise even though she had witnessed a lifetime of well-kept promises. David became an adulterer. Eve did the one thing God asked her not to do.

Many years ago I read a poem called "The Land of Beginning Again." It described a place where we could put aside our failures and problems. That place exists; it is in God's grace. He is willing to give us the chance for a divine comeback, just as He has given this chance to the people in the Bible. We cannot run far enough, disobey long enough, or do anything wrong enough that God does not want us back.

> *We cannot run far enough, disobey long enough, or do anything wrong enough that God does not want us back.*

2. God Gives Us a Second Chance Because Others Need It

God loves us and wants us to be able to begin again, but He also gives us a second chance because of what it can do for others. In Jonah's day, Nineveh was a city of 120,000 people. But the city was wicked and violent, and Jonah knew it. He didn't want God to save those people. He didn't want the Ninevites to receive a second chance. But God wanted to give it to them. He always does. He gave the Ninevites a second chance. He gave the sailors on board the sinking ship a second chance, and He gave Jonah the disobedient a second chance.

I'm grateful for the second chances God has given me. He has always forgiven me when I've done wrong. And He has saved me from death, just as He did Jonah. It was only by God's grace and the skill of two surgeons that I survived the heart attack I had in 1998. Ten years later, I realized how much God had done for other people because He had given me a second chance: More than ten thousand people have given their lives to God. Hundreds of thousands of people have been helped by Catalyst, a conference I founded. Five million leaders have been trained in nearly every country around the world. Many millions more have been helped by the books I've written since 1998. Four thousand John Maxwell Team coaches in 120 countries have started building my legacy. And more than a billion dollars has been raised to help churches in the United States. All these things happened because God gave me a second chance.

If you ask God to give you a second chance, it is not an entirely selfish act. You have no idea how many people you may help if you seek God's forgiveness and obey His calling on your life.

3. God Gives Us a Second Chance Because He Is Good

The bottom line is that it is God's nature to love us, extend us grace, and offer us a second chance. We may fail God, but He will never fail us. The Bible is filled with promise after promise and story after story of God's faithfulness, mercy, and grace when we fall short.

> When we feel tired, God says He will give us rest.[10]
> When we believe we can't go on, God says His grace is enough.[11]
> When we have trouble forgiving ourselves, God says He forgives us.[12]
> When we don't know how we'll make it, God says He will supply all our needs.[13]
> When we can't figure things out, God says He will give us wisdom.[14]
> When we can't make a decision, God says He will direct our steps.[15]

When we feel overwhelmed, God says we can cast all our cares on Him.[16]

For every doubt we have or failure we experience, God has an answer for it that will lead us to a second chance. And though our word to God may fail, God's Word to us does not.

> *For every doubt we have or failure we experience, God has an answer for it that will lead us to a second chance.*

Life Lessons from Jonah

I find myself wondering what Jonah learned from the second chance he received from God. I don't have long to wait before he starts speaking:

"It's Possible to Do the Right Thing with the Wrong Attitude"

"When the giant fish vomited me onto the shore, I couldn't stand my own stench. I cannot tell you how terrible it was to be in the belly of such a sea creature. But as bad as my smell was, my attitude was even worse. I obeyed God, but I hated the people God had me talk to. I was bitter and angry when the Ninevites repented and God gave them a second chance. I was obedient on the outside, but I was still rebellious on the inside.

"I was wrong. I should have celebrated the fact that an entire city received the same grace and loving-kindness I had received. I should have changed my attitude. Instead I sulked. Only now from this perspective am I able to wish that I had seen people the way God sees them, that I had valued people the way He does, that I had loved people the way God does. All people matter to God, and so they should matter to me."

> *All people matter to God, and so they should matter to me.*

"Be Grateful That God Uses Imperfect People"

"God can use anyone—and He does. Thank goodness for that, because imperfect people are the only kind there are. I was so arrogant. I believed that I had a case against God, that He was wrong. When I decided to flee to Tarshish, it did not surprise God. Nor did it prevent Him from exercising His will. He even used my act of disobedience to save the sailors aboard the ship," Jonah says. "Who could have been better to demonstrate the power of God's grace and love than the Ninevites?

"The question that begs asking is why God gave me a second chance. There were others who could have delivered His message. Certainly there were better people among the Israelites who would have obeyed God the first time. But God wasn't looking for a better person." Jonah's gaze becomes piercing. "God was looking for the right one, the person *He* wanted. And I, Jonah, in spite of my problems, in spite of my disobedience, was the person God wanted. To me that is humbling, and I'm so very grateful."

"When You Get a Second Chance—Make It Count"

"When I finally was spit out by the great fish and lay gasping for air on the shore, all I could think at first was, *I'm alive! Thanks be to God that I'm alive.* As I lay there, even before I tried to stand, I knew God was asking me again to go to Nineveh. I was determined to obey, and I did. But it wasn't until later—much later—that I realized the implications of being given a second chance.

"It meant I had failed the first time. We never get another *first* chance. What might my life have been like if I had obeyed the first time? What privileges had I lost? What opportunities had I missed? What impact had I forfeited? Might God have asked me to go to another city? Might others have been saved?

"As these questions rushed into my mind, I became aware of how desperately I needed God's grace. God had spared me. He had not given me what I deserved. Yet even after the Ninevites repented from their wicked ways and turned to God, I still didn't understand. In time God's grace helped to heal my bitterness and change my attitude. It kept inviting me to come back to God in spite of my failure, weakness, and sin. Grace always runs downhill. It met me when I was at the bottom, not the top.

> *Grace always runs downhill. It met me when I was at the bottom, not the top.*

"God wants to extend grace to you too," says Jonah. "When you get a second chance, make it count! No matter what you did in the past, it's not too late for you. If you allow Him to, God will still use you—as imperfect as you are. If God was able to use me with my disobedience, bitterness, and bad attitude, just think what He might be able to do with you."

Jonah's Prayer for Us

I know our time with Jonah is coming to an end when he leans forward and places a hand on each of our arms. I'm surprised to feel that his touch is cold. But his words are warm as he prays for us:

> *"Oh God My Lord Who Is Always There,*
>
> *"Help Your servants to understand Your grace and mercy at a level as deep as the ocean itself. Teach them to make the most of the second chances that You grant. And help them to make the time they have left on this earth count. Amen."*

Leadership Lessons from Jonah

Jonah looks each of us in the eye one more time and nods to us. I feel encouraged by his words. As he departs, I think about his influence and the lessons we can learn from his life:

1. A Leader's Decision Affects Many People

For either good or bad, everything rises and falls on leadership. Every decision Jonah made had an impact on others. When he was making bad choices, it hurt people. His decision to disobey God and get on the ship hurt the sailors. It hurt the merchants whose cargo was thrown overboard. It hurt Jonah himself. And it meant the 120,000 people of Nineveh had to wait longer to hear God's message.

However, when Jonah decided to own up to his dis-obedience and tell the sailors he was the cause of the storm, they learned about God, it saved their lives, and they turned to God afterward. And of course when Jonah got his second chance and decided to go to Nineveh, the people there heard God's message, repented, and were spared God's wrath.

As leaders, we must never forget that every decision we make affects other people. The greater the influence and higher the position, the larger the number of people affected. The decisions of leaders have a compounding effect on others—either positive or negative.

2. Leaders Must Continually Examine Their Hearts

In the end, Jonah obeyed God and fulfilled His will. But Jonah's heart wasn't right, and God called him on it. God didn't want Jonah to hate the people of Nineveh. He wanted him to show them compassion.

Good leaders do the right things for the right reasons with the right heart. For that reason, we must continually examine our hearts. Emotions like anger, fear, resentment, and jealousy do not serve us well. They misplace our motives and taint our judgment.

I want to be a good leader. I'm sure you do too. That means being motivated by the same things that motivate God: love, joy, peace, patience, goodness, kindness, faithfulness, gentleness, and self-control.

To examine our hearts, we need to ask ourselves whether we've sought God's will for any given situation. We need to consider if He would be pleased with our words and actions. We need to try to see things from His perspective.

3. God Chooses to Work Through Leaders to Help Others

One of the things that strikes me about Jonah's story is how much He wanted to use Jonah to fulfill His purpose. God could have sent an angel to the people of Nineveh, yet He instead chose a human leader. And even when that leader disobeyed and failed, God still wanted to use him.

Several years ago I wrote down the top ten questions I wanted to ask God when I arrived in heaven. One of those questions was "Why did You choose people to fulfill Your purpose, and why did You pick some of the people You did?" When I think about how God chose me, I become completely overwhelmed! I know that if I were in charge of the universe, I would not choose me to reach other people, because I know how weak I am in my human-ness. And I certainly would not give me the amount of influence God has entrusted to me. Still today, I marvel at God's decision to do work through me. It daily fills my heart with gratitude.

Jonah's Discussion Guide

Then the word of the Lord came to Jonah a second time: "Go to the great city of Nineveh and proclaim to it the message I give you."

Jonah obeyed the word of the Lord and went to Nineveh. Now Nineveh was a very large city; it took three days to go through it. Jonah began by going a day's journey into the city, proclaiming, "Forty more days and Nineveh will be overthrown." The Ninevites believed God. A fast was proclaimed, and all of them, from the greatest to the least, put on sackcloth....

When God saw what they did and how they turned from their evil ways, he relented and did not bring on them the destruction he had threatened. (Jonah 3:1–5, 10)

1. People today may tend to think it's quaint that Jonah tried to get away from God by getting on a ship. But what methods do people use today to avoid or escape God?

2. Have you ever known people who did the right things but with the wrong attitude? If so, describe how that

negatively affected them as well as the people around them.

3. When someone treats you badly or does something wrong to you, how difficult do you find it to forgive him or her?

4. Do you intuitively believe it's God's nature to give people second chances? Explain.

5. Do you find it easy or difficult to accept that God is willing to use imperfect people to fulfill His will? Do you have a harder time with that concept when it's applied to you or to others? Explain.

6. In what area of life would you most like to have a second chance? Why?

7. What will need to happen for you to move forward in that area and make your second chance count?

To learn more about Jonah, read 2 Kings 14:25 and Jonah 1:1–4:11.

JOSHUA

*God Is Greater than Your Greatest
Challenges*

It's getting to be late in the afternoon. My study is on the east side of the house, and the sun has moved down the sky in the west. The light is getting cooler. The day has been rushing by.

Soon we hear the steady deliberate tread of someone walking up the hallway. The man who walks through the doorway looks like he has stepped out of an action movie. He's powerfully built and appears to be in the prime of life. A sheathed sword hangs at his side.

He strides over to the chair opposite us, and before he sits down, he detaches his sword. He lays it on the floor beside his chair. I notice that he positions it within easy reach. I suspect the scabbard could be in his hand and the sword unsheathed from it in mere seconds. Clearly this man is a warrior.

"I was born a slave," he says, "in the land of Egypt. I wandered in the desert for forty years because of the disobedience of God's people. But because I was faithful to God and was willing the first time when God asked, when it was time again to enter the Promised Land, God chose me to lead the children of Israel across the Jordan."

This is undoubtedly Joshua. "My life was a series of challenges," Joshua continues. "I started life in chains, but God did not leave me there. He broke every chain that tried to hold me down. You need to understand something: *God is greater than your greatest challenges.*"

Unchained

I once read a quote by Emmet Fox that said, "It is the Law that any difficulties that can come to you at any time, no matter what they are, must be exactly what you need most at the moment, to enable you to take the next step forward by overcoming them. The only real misfortune, the only real tragedy, comes when we suffer without learning the lesson." When we fail to meet those challenges, we fail to meet our potential. Joshua did not have that problem. He was someone who met the challenges he faced with courage and faith, and God broke the chains so he could reach his potential.

I try to imagine what it would be like to have been born a slave. It would mean never being able to make your own decisions. Never being able to own property. Never having the promise of a better future. That's where Joshua started. But God intervened. He heard the cries of His people and broke the chains of bondage for Joshua and all the other children of Israel.

It must have been with great hope that Joshua and the other Israelites set off from Egypt for the land flowing with milk and honey. After seeing God part the Red Sea and destroy Pharaoh's army, they must have understood that God Himself was leading them. Perhaps this was why Joshua wasn't afraid to go down and fight the Amalekites when Moses told him to. At that time Joshua was no warrior. He had no battle experience. He was a leader of his family, but he had been a lifelong slave. The only thing he had going for him was a relationship with Moses, a leader he had served since he was a boy. Moses knew God would intervene, and Joshua trusted Moses. And God gave Joshua victory. As long as Moses's hands were raised in prayer, Joshua prevailed. He and his men defeated the Amalekites so thoroughly that God asked Moses to write down the story so it could be remembered.

After that it should be no surprise that Joshua was one of the twelve spies chosen to explore the Promised

Land. When he and Caleb came back from their trip, they were both ready to take the land. But the rest of their company was still in chains, mentally and emotionally, if not physically. They believed it would be easier to stay in the comfort of the desert than to face the unknown in the Promised Land. The more the people complained, the greater the doubt that grew in their hearts—and the bigger the challenges became in their eyes. They saw themselves as grasshoppers in comparison to their enemies. It's hard to lead grasshoppers to victory.

So the entire generation of former slaves kept themselves in bondage. They wandered in the desert for forty years. And Joshua had to wait for every one of that generation to die except Caleb and himself before God called them again to cross into the Promised Land. And this time it would be Joshua, not Moses, who was asked to lead the nation forward.

Life Lessons from Joshua

As we wait to hear Joshua speak, I think about how as a child in the fourth grade, I started to understand some of the privileges of leadership. On the playground I would pick certain kids to play on my team. The better I selected, the better the odds were of winning the game.

Joshua didn't get to pick his own team to lead into the Promised Land. Nor did he get to pick the time they crossed over or the strategy for conquering it. He had to defeat armies, destroy cities, and take territory while leading people with no skills or experience. And he had to do all this without Moses, his leader and mentor.

My reverie is broken as Joshua begins to speak:

"When Moses died, I knew I would not be able to fill his shoes. There will never be another like him," Joshua says. "But God told me to take the land, and I knew He was with me. So I moved forward. And so should you, even when you feel the challenge is too great.

"My friends, do not get discouraged when you feel overwhelmed. Instead, remember to do these things with God's help…"

"Rise Above Your Past Failures"

"An entire generation of my people died in the desert because I could not convince them to enter the Promised Land," says Joshua. "My influence was so weak, they ignored my pleas. They said they would rather die in the desert, or worse yet, return to Egypt to become slaves again. They became so enraged that they threatened to stone me. It was at that time I realized my leadership had very little influence over the people.

"How was I to do something that even the great Moses could not accomplish? It seemed impossible. But I was the leader! I had to move forward from the place of my biggest failure.

"It was at that moment that I realized my failure didn't define me or determine my future. God's will and my obedience would.

"I stepped forward determined not to confuse a single defeat with a final defeat. And just as Moses was able to see the Promised Land from Mount Pisgah before he died, I was able to rise above my failure.

> *One plus God is always a majority.*

"One plus God is always a majority," says Joshua. "Do not allow past failures to keep you from future successes. God is greater than that."

"Claim the Promises God Has for You"

"God will never go back on a promise He makes," says Joshua. "God originally promised to give the land to my ancestor, Abraham. And He reaffirmed that promise to Abraham's children, grandchildren, and great-grandchildren. The land was our inheritance. All we had to do was take it. The first time, we didn't do that.

"But God didn't give up on us. He gave me a second

chance, and with me He gave one to the nation of Israel," Joshua continues. "And He gave additional promises to me personally. He said He would be with me. He told me that no one would be able to stand up against me. However, there was one promise given to me as a leader that I did not fully act upon. God said He would give me every bit of land I placed my foot on. The Promised Land contained three hundred thousand square miles, yet I only claimed thirty thousand—just 10 percent!

"We are given only what we are willing to claim. The extent of our victory was limited by our faith, not God's promises."

"Obey God and Do What You Can Do"

"Crossing over into the Promised Land was a great challenge, one that looked impossible at the time. The Jordan is a powerful river, a mile wide at the point where God directed us to cross. And I had to take two million people beyond it without boats or bridges.

"God's instructions to us were to move forward, and I was determined that we would not falter again," says Joshua. His face is stern. His gaze is strong. His will seems to be made of iron. "So we prepared ourselves. I told the people to sanctify themselves. They were to examine themselves, make themselves as clean and holy as possible, and put away anything that might be displeasing to God. That was within our power. It was also within our power to follow God.

"I told the people that we had never been on this road before," says Joshua. "When Moses parted the Red Sea, the pathway was clear and the water was gone before we took a step. But this time God was asking us to take the step first. Maybe that was because we had failed the first time. But who knows? You cannot put God in a box.

"When God asks you to take a step," Joshua states, "don't hesitate. Do what you can do, even if you are uncertain of the outcome."

"Trust God to Do What You Cannot Do"

"Sure enough, when the priests carrying the Ark stepped into the shallows of the Jordan, the water stopped flowing. Upstream the water piled up in a heap for twenty miles," says Joshua. "God had done the impossible—again.

"God responds to our obedience," says Joshua. "If we want God to help us with our greatest challenges, we must do what He asks. Without God, we cannot. Without us, God will not! We want God to fix everything in our lives *for* us. He would rather

> Without God, we cannot. Without us, God will not.

come alongside and work *with* us. For that reason the challenges in life will never stop. It is God's way of keeping us close to Him.

"I remembered that as we took the Promised Land, just as God had told us we could. I was wise to trust God. You would be too.

"Trust God when challenges confront you;
Trust Him when your faith is too small.
Trust Him when simply to trust Him
Is the hardest thing of all."

Joshua's Prayer for Us

Without missing a beat, Joshua begins to pray for us, his strong deep voice becoming more gentle as he speaks:

"Oh Lord my Banner,

"Strengthen my friends. Give them courage and strength. Help them to know that You will never abandon them or forsake them. Assure them that Your promises are true. When they face great challenges, help them to know in their heart of hearts that Your care is even greater. And give them the confidence to achieve Your victories. Amen."

Leadership Lessons from Joshua

When Joshua is finished speaking, he reaches for his sword and stands easily to his feet. As he departs, I think about how there are so many leadership lessons we can learn from this great commander:

1. Let God Encourage You with Courage

The core of leadership is courage. Joshua needed a way to find courage within himself so he could encourage others. This was no small feat, because he had failed in the past, and he was forced to live with that failure for forty years.

The severity of a problem lies not in how difficult it is to deal with. It lies in whether it's the same problem you had yesterday, last month, and last year. How about having to deal with a problem that had existed for as long as all your people had been alive? But God helped Joshua. Scripture records that God encouraged the people eleven times in eleven chapters. Why so often? Because one word of encouragement was not sufficient for forty years of failure.

2. Keep God in the Picture

Too often our problems are pictures without God in them. I learned this when I was visited by legendary NFL linebacker Mike Singletary and we had lunch together. When he was about to leave, he asked if he could have a picture with me. I was blown

> *Too often our problems are pictures without God in them.*

away. I thought, *I should be asking to be in a picture with you!* That's the way God feels about us. *He* wants to be in the picture with me. He wants to be in the picture with you. Let's not keep Him out of it.

Just as God had promised Moses that He would stay in the picture, God promised the same thing to Joshua. When Joshua got ready to cross the Jordan River, God was in the forefront of his mind and in everyone else's. Joshua asked them to keep their eyes on the Ark, the representation of God's presence and His seat when the Ark was in the holy of holies. It was their reminder that God was in the picture with them.

As leaders, we must find ways to keep God in the picture. We need to do it visually. We need to do it creatively. And we need to do it continually.

3. Focus on the Possibilities, Not the Problem

Most people are problem spotters instead of problem solvers. Leaders cannot think that way if they want to be successful. The other ten spies didn't learn this. When they explored the Promised Land, all they saw were the challenges. They spotted giants. They felt small. They became afraid. They forgot all about the possibilities God had spoken of when He promised Abraham's descendents the land. Joshua and Caleb never let the obstacles outweigh the opportunities.

> *Joshua and Caleb never let the obstacles outweigh the opportunities.*

As you face challenges, it doesn't matter how great the problems are if the possibilities are greater. Keep your focus on what's important. You need to do that not only for yourself, but also for the people you lead.

Joshua's Discussion Guide

All the Israelites grumbled against Moses and Aaron, and the whole assembly said to them, "If only we had died in Egypt! Or in this wilderness!..." And they said to each other, "We should choose a leader and go back to Egypt."

Then Moses and Aaron fell facedown in front of the whole Israelite assembly gathered there. Joshua son of Nun and Caleb son of Jephunneh, who were among those who had explored the land, tore their clothes and said to the entire Israelite assembly, "The land we passed through and explored is exceedingly good. If the Lord is pleased with us, he will lead us into that land, a land flowing with milk and honey, and will give it to us. Only do not rebel against the Lord. And do not be afraid of the people of the land, because we will devour them. Their protection is gone, but the Lord is with us. Do not be afraid of them." (Numbers 14:2, 4–9)

1. What do you think it would have been like to be a slave in Egypt and then gain your freedom?

2. Why do you think the Israelites would have preferred to move back to Egypt than to move forward into the Promised Land? Do you relate to them or not? Why?

3. Joshua had to overcome past failures to do what God was asking of him. What failures has God helped you overcome?

4. Can you recall a time when God came through for you personally, if not as dramatically as He did by parting the Red Sea or providing manna?

5. Do you naturally tend to see problems or possibilities? Why?

6. What Scriptures or stories from the Bible help you to gain courage? Explain.

7. Joshua asked the people to keep their eyes on the Ark to remind them of God. What do you do to remind yourself of God's role in your life?

8. What challenge is God currently asking you to overcome, and what act of obedience does He want you to perform in order to move forward?

To learn more about Joshua, read Exodus 17:8–16, 32:17–18, and 33:7–11, Numbers 11:28, 13:1–14:38, and 27:12–23, Deuteronomy 1:37–38, 3:21–22, 3:28, 31:7–8, 31:14, and 34:1–12, and Joshua 1:1–24:33.

DANIEL

Have a Purpose Bigger than You

The sun is low in the sky. My eastward-facing study is now mostly in shadow. There is perhaps a little more than an hour of daylight left, and I realize there is time for only one more person to visit us.

The footfalls we hear from the hallway are soft, barely audible. It makes me wonder what kind of shoes the person is wearing. When the figure appears from around the corner, I see that he is wearing shoes made of a fine gold-colored fabric. A bright-red robe, edged with gold tassels, hangs down almost to his feet. A sash hangs over one shoulder and down at an angle across his chest. It is made of fine gold-colored fabric like the shoes and tassels.

And then I look up and see his face. Even though he has a long dark beard, I can see that this man is strikingly handsome. Movie-star handsome. He wears a gold band around his head that has some sort of symbol on the front of it. And he's tall. I have to look up to look him in the eye.

As the man sits in the chair opposite us, I notice that he carries a rod about a foot and a half long. It appears to be made of gold. On his hand is an enormous gold ring with an intricate seal. It looks like it may feature the same symbol that is on his headband. Is this a king? Some kind of official? Who is it?

"When I was taken into captivity, I did not know what would happen to me," he says. "I had lived like a prince, but I became a slave. I wondered if I would be forced to work in a mine or if they would sacrifice me to some pagan god.

"We were forced to go to Babylon, thousands of us. The road was a long one. The journey took us over five months," he continues, "and many of my people died along the way, including my parents and siblings. When we finally arrived, we found Babylon to be an inhospitable place—huge and alien. Many of us would rather have died in Jerusalem.

"I was astounded when the chief of the court officials chose me and three of my friends to be trained for the king's service. For three years they prepared us, teaching us to speak and write in their language, making us study their literature, educating us in all of their ways," he says.

"But I was resolved. It did not matter what my captors did to me. I would not give up or give in. I would not defile myself. Nor would I bow down to pagan gods. My name is Daniel, and I was determined to live for something greater. And that is my advice to you," he says. *"Have a purpose bigger than you."*

Greater than Rulers or Empires

Scripture says that Daniel was among the best and brightest of the Hebrews and was chosen along with three other young men from the tribe of Judah to be part of the court of Nebuchadnezzar, ruler of the Babylonian Empire. Some people might have refused and been executed. Others might have compromised and become Babylonian in spirit as well as action. Daniel and his friends— Hananiah, Mishael, and Azariah—took another course. They remained true to a higher purpose. They sought to glorify God by serving with excellence the king who had made them slaves.

Daniel's sense of purpose did many things for him...

1. Purpose Gave Him Clarity

Being chosen for special treatment by his captors must have been confusing to Daniel. Feelings of resentment for the people who had conquered his nation must have been mixed with the hope of a better life. Would he let his loyalty and grief drive him to bitterness? Or would he be grateful for a chance at making a difference? It would be easy for someone in his position to lose his way.

Danish philosopher Søren Kierkegaard remarked, "What I really lack is to be clear in my mind what I am to do, not what I am to know....The thing is to understand myself, to see what God really wishes me to do...to find the idea for which I can live and die." Daniel and his friends found that idea: they would be faithful to God and make the most of the opportunity they were being given.

2. Purpose Gave Him Conviction

When Daniel and his friends were offered food from the king's table, which would have caused them to violate the dietary laws they had always followed, they had a choice to make. Would they bow to convenience, or stand upon conviction? They chose conviction. They decided that they would not defile themselves. That was a great risk, because if their actions did not bring positive results in the eyes of their captors, it meant death for all of them, including their guards.

They stood for what was right, knowing they would win even if they lost. They had certain values that would sustain them in defeat or in victory. And these values, tested by passion, were convictions. These four young men were not drab, lifeless people who blended in with the crowd. People with convictions never are.

3. Purpose Gave Him Confidence

There are two levels of confidence for people of faith: self-confidence and God-confidence. Self-confidence comes from knowing and trusting yourself. God-confidence comes from knowing and trusting God. Self-confidence plus God-confidence equals Daniel-confidence.

When Daniel refused the king's food and suggested an alternative course of action to the official and the guard in charge of him, I don't believe he was rolling the dice. I believe he was confident that honoring God would bring positive results.

The official in charge of Daniel and his friends was afraid of Nebuchadnezzar, and with good reason: the king could have him executed for not following orders. But the favor of God and the confidence of Daniel won over the official, and he allowed Daniel and the other three to eat only vegetables and drink nothing but water. And that confidence paid off. After ten days, the four young Hebrews looked healthier and better nourished than any of the young men who had eaten the king's food.

Life Lessons from Daniel

The stories of people like Daniel remind us that God has a purpose for each of us, if only we will seek it. We just need to obey what God asks us to do and be faithful to Him.

I can't help but admire Daniel, and I can't wait to hear what wisdom he wishes to impart to us.

"When Your Purpose Is Bigger Than You, It Will Set You Apart from the Crowd"

"Yes, it's true that we were selected from the exiles because we were physically strong, intelligent, and able to learn," Daniel says. "That was true of all the young men who were selected from among the Israelites. But we stood out even among them because we sensed that God had a bigger purpose for us and we stood up for God. That was true when we chose not to eat the king's choice food. And it was even more obvious when my three friends, who became known as Shadrach, Meshach, and

Abednego, refused to bow down to an idol. In punishment, they were thrown into the fiery furnace—but God saved them! Their example became a testimony of God's greatness. And the three were rewarded by being given greater influence in Babylon.

"When you follow a purpose that is bigger than you are, it makes you stand out from the crowd. Some people will see that and attack you for it. Do not compromise," says Daniel fiercely. "Be yourself and remain true to God—when the temptation is to go with the crowd, when your integrity is put to the test, when the rest of the world begs you to be someone else. Be true to yourself and true to God, and He will be glorified."

"When Your Purpose Is Bigger Than You, It Will Require God's Favor"

"When your purpose is no greater than yourself, it's easy for you to rely on only yourself. But when your purpose is bigger, you need God's favor to accomplish it. When you are asked to do the impossible, as I was, it requires God to do a miracle.

> *When your purpose is no greater than yourself, it's easy for you to rely on only yourself. But when your purpose is bigger, you need God's favor to accomplish it.*

"King Nebuchadnezzar had a dream and asked his astrologers to not only interpret the dream, but tell him what the dream had been. They deemed his request impossible for any human being. And they were right. But it was not impossible for God. When my three friends and I prayed, God solved the mystery and revealed the answer.

"When you submit yourself to God and tap into His purpose for your life, He will ask you to do things you are incapable of doing. Don't let that dissuade you from following Him. Greatness doesn't come from doing all you can do. It comes from allowing God to do all He can do *through* you."

> *Greatness doesn't come from doing all you can do. It comes from allowing God to do all He can do through you.*

"When Your Purpose Is Bigger Than You, It Will Give You Courage"

"The longer you walk with God and strive to live according to His greater purpose, the more courage He will give you to fulfill His will," Daniel explains. "When the satraps conspired against me to have me put in the lion's den, I was no longer a young man. I had served Nebuchadnezzar until his death, and by that time I was serving my third king. Knowing I prayed to God three times a day, these corrupt officials tricked King Darius into establishing a decree that for thirty days, if anyone was found to be praying to anyone but the king, that person would be fed to the lions.

"When they threw me to the lions, they thought they had beaten me. But I did not lose hope. Just as God had given me His favor, He gave me courage. And God answered my prayer by sending an angel to protect me. In the end, it was they who got fed to the lions.

"I discovered over time that courage is like a muscle: it is strengthened by use. Each time I made a courageous decision, I developed that muscle. If you seek God's bigger purpose and choose to follow Him, He will give you the courage you need to fulfill the tasks He gives you."

"When Your Purpose Is Bigger Than You, It Will Be Tested"

"When you choose to follow a bigger purpose, it's not a one-time decision. Your resolve will be tested. If you want to finish well, you must keep choosing to follow God," says Daniel.

"When they wanted me

> *When you choose to follow a bigger purpose, it's not a one-time decision. Your resolve will be tested.*

to eat the wrong foods, I had to choose to follow God. When they asked me to interpret the dream, I had to choose to follow God. When I spoke hard truths to the kings, I had to choose to follow God. And when I faced the lions, I had to choose to follow God.

"When your time of testing comes, make the right decision. Choose God! I was able to do that continually because my purpose was not for myself. It was for God."

Daniel's Prayer for Us

"Lord God Most High,

"I know You have a purpose for these friends. Reveal it to them in a deeper way. Give them the clarity to know it, the conviction to fulfill it, the confidence to invite others into it with them, and the courage needed when the times of testing come. May Your will be done through them. Amen."

Leadership Lessons from Daniel

Daniel's words give us strength and hope. God desires to do important things through us. What He chooses may not look important to the world. At times it may not even seem important to us. But if it matters to God, it is important.

Daniel's life is also a reminder that to lead for God, a person need not be born into an important family, possess riches, or have a title or position. Daniel started his career as a slave. And he died a slave. But what he did in his lifetime made an impact.

Three leadership lessons stand out from Daniel's life:

1. God Chooses the Purpose Before the Person

When I think of how Daniel's life and leadership unfolded, I am reminded of the words God gave to Jeremiah: "Before I formed you in the womb I knew you, before you were born I set you apart; I appointed you as a prophet to the nations."[17]

Look at how God worked in Jeremiah's life: first He knew who He wanted Jeremiah to be. Then God formed him in his mother's womb, giving him a unique set of strengths and weaknesses to match the significant calling on his life. He was specifically designed for his unique purpose.

The same was true for Daniel. And the same is true for us. God's purpose for us was in place before we were born. God's favor has been available to use from the beginning. God created us to do good works, which He prepared in advance for us to do.[18] That means He made us to serve, to influence, to make a difference. We only need to be willing to follow Him as He leads us toward that purpose. The gap between making a difference and making no difference at all isn't talent, opportunity, or privilege. It's purpose. People who fail to make a difference in the lives of others lack purpose.

2. When Leaders Follow God's Purpose, They Are Given God's Power

Daniel served four kings from two different conquering empires. More than once he was asked to do the impossible. With God's help, he was able to do it. And God was always honored.

When God gives leaders something to do according to His purpose, He provides them with the power and favor they need to complete it. If you are pursuing the bigger purpose of doing what God created you to do, He will provide the resources you need.

3. On-Purpose Leaders Do the Right Thing—Not the Easy Thing

Daniel did not live a stress-free life. He was a slave living in exile. He was at the whim of arrogant kings. He was surrounded by jealous court officials who plotted against him and tried to have him killed. Yet Daniel never lost his way—because he never

> *Daniel never lost his way—because he never lost his why.*

lost his why. His vision was to honor God in everything he did. And he was successful.

As a leader, your why needs to be bigger than you are. If you are bigger than your why, you might have a successful career, but you will have little more. However, if your why is bigger than you are, you have a calling. And your calling makes it possible for you to always do the right thing, not merely the easy thing.

It's said that there are two great days in every person's life: the day you are born...and the day you discover why. If you know your why and follow that bigger purpose, all the other little whys will fall into place, and you will be able to do the things you were created to do, as Daniel was.

Daniel's Discussion Guide

The king asked Daniel (also called Belteshazzar), "Are you able to tell me what I saw in my dream and interpret it?"

Daniel replied, "No wise man, enchanter, magician or diviner can explain to the king the mystery he has asked about, but there is a God in heaven who reveals mysteries. He has shown King Nebuchadnezzar what will happen in days to come. Your dream and the visions that passed through your mind as you were lying in bed are these:..."

Then King Nebuchadnezzar fell prostrate before Daniel and paid him honor and ordered that an offering and incense be presented to him. The king said to Daniel, "Surely your God is the God of gods and the Lord of kings and a revealer of mysteries, for you were able to reveal this mystery."

Then the king placed Daniel in a high position and lavished many gifts on him. He made him ruler over the entire province of Babylon and placed him in charge of all its wise men. Moreover, at Daniel's request the king appointed Shadrach, Meshach and Abednego administrators over the province of Babylon, while Daniel himself remained at the royal court. (Daniel 2:26–28, 46–49)

1. How easy or difficult do you find it to relate to Daniel and his three friends' standing up for what they believe? Explain.
2. Do you believe everyone who follows God is set apart by Him, or do you think only certain people are? Explain.
3. Scripture says that God created us to do good works, which He prepared in advance for us to do. Do you have a sense of the kinds of things God created you to do? If so, what are they?
4. What kinds of things have you done in the past to try to understand and identify your purpose?
5. How do you handle fear when you believe God wants you to do something, but you are afraid to do it?
6. Where would you like to experience more of God's power and favor in your life?
7. What specific step or action do you believe you need to take to experience it?

To learn more about Daniel, read Daniel 1:1–12:13.

END OF DAY

The eastern sky over the water is dark, and we can barely see the horizon. But up higher in the sky there is a soft glow, the last bit of light before the sun goes down. The sound of Daniel's footsteps slowly fades away as he walks down the hall, and then it's silent.

I have no idea how long we sit there. When I snap out of my reverie, I realize the sun is gone and the study is completely dark.

Scripture says that after Moses would meet with God in the tent outside the camp, Joshua, who was his aide at the time, would stay in the tent after Moses left it. I think I know how Joshua felt. I have no desire to leave this spot. I want the experience to continue, but I know the time has passed.

I think about the giants of the faith we met today, and the messages they had for us:

Elijah: God loves you on your bad days.

Elisha: Give your best wherever God puts you.

Job: God sees the big picture.

Jacob: Let God have control of your life.

Deborah: God specializes in the unexpected.

Isaiah: God has a reason for your encounter with Him.

Jonah: God always gives us a second chance.

Joshua: God is greater than your greatest challenges.

Daniel: Have a purpose bigger than yourself.

The thought of them makes me smile.

We can't avoid it any longer; it's time for us to go. We get up from our seats. You go your way, refreshed and strengthened for the journey ahead. I take one more look around my study. And before I walk out, I think, *It's been a good day.*

NOTES

1. Randy Alcorn, "The Leader's Character; Leadership is a privilege, not an entitlement," http://www.epm.org/blog/2009/Feb/26/the-leaders-character-leadership-is-a-privilege-no, accessed February 13, 2014.

2. Genesis 28:20–22.

3. Mark 8:35.

4. C. S. Lewis, *Mere Christianity* (New York: HarperOne, 2001), 205.

5. Genesis 25:23.

6. Isaiah 6:3.

7. Isaiah 6:5.

8. Isaiah 6:8.

9. 2 Kings 20:1–7.

10. Matthew 11:28–30.

11. 2 Corinthians 12:9.

12. 1 John 1:9.

13. Philippians 4:19.

14. James 1:5.

15. Proverbs 3:5–6.

16. 1 Peter 5:7.

17. Jeremiah 1:5.

18. Ephesians 2:10.

Look for John C. Maxwell's bestselling book

RUNNING WITH THE GIANTS
What the Old Testament Heroes Want You to Know About Life and Leadership

From David to Abraham, Moses to Rebekah, John Maxwell puts you face-to-face with towering figures of the Old Testament and shares the lessons you can learn from them about life, leadership, and yourself. Available now in print, electronic, and audio formats from FaithWords wherever books are sold.

And coming in spring 2015

WALKING WITH THE GIANTS
Lessons on Life and Leadership from Women in the Bible

John C. Maxwell delivers more valuable insights on life and leadership drawn specifically from the lives of some of the most influential biblical women.